What's God Got to Do with It?

What's God Got to Do with It?

ROBERT INGERSOLL
*on Free Thought, Honest Talk, and the
Separation of Church and State*

Edited and with an introduction by
TIM PAGE

STEERFORTH PRESS
HANOVER, NEW HAMPSHIRE

For information about permission to reproduce
selections from this book, write to:
Steerforth Press L.C., 25 Lebanon Street
Hanover, New Hampshire 03755

Frontispiece photograph of Robert Ingersoll appears courtesy
robertingersoll.com

Library of Congress Cataloging-in-Publication Data
Ingersoll, Robert Green, 1833–1899.
  What's God got to do with it? : Robert G. Ingersoll on free thought,
honest talk, and the separation of church and state / edited and with
an introduction by Tim Page. — 1st ed.
      p. cm.
  Includes bibliographical references.
  ISBN 1-58642-096-8 (alk. paper)
  1. Agnosticism. 2. Free thought. 3. Church and states — United
States. I. Page, Tim, 1954– II. Title.
  BL2720.A2I55 2005
  211'.7–dc22

                                    2005010101

FIRST EDITION

While I am opposed to all orthodox creeds, I have a creed myself; and my creed is this. Happiness is the only good. The time to be happy is now. The place to be happy is here. The way to be happy is to make others so. This creed is somewhat short, but it is long enough for this life, strong enough for this world. If there is another world, when we get there we can make another creed. But this creed certainly will do for this life.

Robert Green Ingersoll, 1882

ROBERT INGERSOLL

He was an impassioned patriot, an early member of the Republican Party, and a supporter of Abraham Lincoln. He was a tireless advocate for justice and liberty, a man who thought the Declaration of Independence the "bravest, grandest" political document ever conceived. He spoke out on most of the great issues of his day — race relations, women's rights, birth control, capital punishment, the role of religion in a modern state — with a combination of moral authority and mischievous wit. The power of his ideas and his skills as an orator made him one of the most famous men in America. And today — in an era of "faith-based initiatives" and White House prayer breakfasts, at a time when "televangelists" attack children's cartoon characters for supposed homosexual tendencies and evolution is downgraded to a mere theory, one out of many, in textbooks — the wisdom of Colonel Robert Ingersoll (1833–1899) is as resonant and relevant as ever.

Ingersoll is one of the great lost totemic figures in American history, and it is time that he was brought back into our collective consciousness. After Ralph Waldo Emerson, he may have been the busiest and most controversial lecturer of the nineteenth century, attracting many thousands of listeners across the country over the course of each year. His works were published in twelve volumes; he has been the subject of half a dozen biographies; he was a hero to Frederick Douglass, Elizabeth Cady Stanton, and Thomas Edison (who recorded Ingersoll's speaking voice on early wax cylinders). Oscar Wilde called him the most intelligent man in America. Mark Twain praised one of his speeches as "the supreme combination of words that was ever put together since the world began," and added, "Bob Ingersoll's music will sing through my memory always as the divinest that ever enchanted my ears." And H. L. Mencken, writing in the 1920s, suggested that "what this grand, gaudy, unapproachable country needs and lacks is an Ingersoll":

> He drew immense crowds; he became eminent; he planted seeds of infidelity that still sprout in Harvard and Yale. Thousands abandoned their accustomed places of worship to listen to his appalling heresies, and great numbers of them never went back.

Appalling heresies. In these two words lies the secret of Ingersoll's disappearance from view. Although he called himself an agnostic, he was usually labeled an atheist and — except when he was exercising unusual tenderness with an audience's sensibilities — he scarcely seemed to recognize the distinction. And Ingersoll was hardly the sort of quiet, respectful doubter who is still found in every city and town across the nation. Instead, he roared out his skepticism in sharp, lively, cadenced oratory on platforms from Maine to California. His speeches and articles carried aggressively provocative titles such as "Some Mistakes of Moses" and "Why I Am an Agnostic."

Ingersoll was particularly opposed to any attempt to meld church and state, which he considered an erosion of the secular principles set down by the Founding Fathers. He knew that the omission of any reference to God in the United States Constitution was no mere oversight but the result of a consensus — accepted and agreed to by even those among the framers who were deeply religious — that it was dangerous, and unworkable, to incorporate any formal acknowledgment of the supernatural into this fledgling experiment in democracy:

Suppose, then, that we amend the Constitution and acknowledge the existence and supremacy of God — what becomes of the supremacy of the people, and how is this amendment to be enforced? A constitution does not enforce itself. It must be carried out by appropriate legislation.

Will it be a crime to deny the existence of this constitutional God? Can the offender be proceeded against in the criminal courts? Can his lips be closed by the power of the state? Would not this be the inauguration of religious persecution?

Orthodox religionists despised Ingersoll, of course, all the more so as local infamy begat widespread fame. He was denounced from pulpits and editorial pages as a cynic, a rogue, as the Devil himself. His books were banned from libraries; his speeches were regularly disrupted. In 1881, the chief justice of the Delaware Supreme Court went so far as to threaten Ingersoll with indictment under local blasphemy laws (a threat that Ingersoll took seriously enough to cancel all further visits to the "First State").

Despite it all, Ingersoll was an enormously popular attraction and made a handsome living from his tours. And with good reason — even those who disagreed with him most strenuously often found themselves stimulated by the vigor of his arguments and charmed by his humor, which was both daring and self-deprecatory. As the Progressive Senator Robert M. ("Fighting Bob") LaFollette recalled, "He was witty; he was droll; he was eloquent; he was as full of sentiment as an old violin."

When Ingersoll died, when he was no longer around to proclaim his thoughts in person, much of his magic died as well. Moreover, he belongs to that not-inconsequential roster of artists and writers who never created a polished masterpiece. Rather, he returned to the same ideas again and again, in lecture after lecture, with the result that his collected works might qualify for inclusion in what the Firesign Theatre dubbed the "Department of Redundancy Department." But he does not deserve his present obscurity: If Ingersoll is best sifted for nuggets rather than read straight through, the best of those nuggets remain potent and timely.

> The ignorant are not satisfied with what can be demonstrated. Science is too slow for them, and so they invent creeds. They

demand completeness. A sublime segment, a grand fragment, are of no value to them. They demand the complete circle — the entire structure. (Ingersoll in 1877)

Some chips from a "grand fragment," then: Robert Green Ingersoll was born on August 11, 1833, in Dresden, a tiny hamlet in the Finger Lakes region of upstate New York. (The birthplace has been preserved and restored by the Council for Secular Humanism, which runs it as a museum in the summer months.) The boy was the youngest of five children born to Mary Livingston Ingersoll and her husband, John, a Congregational minister. Although Ingersoll was only two years old when his mother died on December 26, 1835, he remembered the event vividly and wrote of it on several occasions. "Nearly forty-eight years ago, under the snow, in the little town of Cazenovia, my poor mother was buried," begins one passage from 1883. "I remember her as she looked in death. That sweet, cold face has kept my heart warm through all the changing years."

His relationship with the melancholy John Ingersoll was necessarily more complicated: "My father whipped his children to keep them out of hell," he recalled. And yet he considered his father "a man of great natural tenderness" who "loved his children almost to insanity. The little severity he had was produced by his religion." Still, these beatings had a wrenching effect on Ingersoll, and in an era when rods were rarely spared, he spoke out movingly against corporal punishment:

> If any one of you ever expects to whip your children again, I want you to have a photograph taken of yourself when you are in the act, with your face red with vulgar anger, and the face of the little child, with eyes swimming in tears and the little chin dimpled with fear.

The family drifted westward, through a dozen or more congregations across New York, Ohio, Wisconsin, and Illinois; Ingersoll grew up immersed in the full intensity of religious fundamentalism:

> After the sermon we had an intermission. Then came the catechism with the chief end of man. We went through with that. We sat in a row with our feet coming in about six inches of the floor. The minister asked us if we knew that we all deserved to go to hell, and we all

answered "Yes." Then we were asked if we
would be willing to go to hell if it was God's
will, and every little liar shouted "Yes."

By the time he was nineteen, Ingersoll had left
home and thrown over scripture for the humanism
of Shakespeare and Burns, who remained his lit-
erary idols for the rest of his life. He settled in the
town of Mount Vernon, Illinois, where he taught
school and studied for the bar, which admitted him
in December 1854. He set up practice with his
brother Ebon, as Ingersoll and Ingersoll, first in the
village of Shawneetown and then in Peoria, the
second-largest city in the state. The brothers spe-
cialized in criminal law.

A fellow lawyer, George Foster, has left a vibrant
picture of the young Robert: "He played with words
as a child plays with flowers, an artist with the keys
of a piano. His voice now painted a word picture of
tender thoughts, now sent forth grand harmonies
that shook the souls of strong men and insensibly
drew them closer and closer still to this matchless
orator."

Ingersoll quickly made a name for himself and
in 1860, at the age of twenty-seven, he ran for
Congress on the Democratic ticket. His defeat was

due in part to his vehement denunciations of the Fugitive Slave Act, a position that put him at odds with party regulars. When the Civil War broke out, Ingersoll helped found the 11th Illinois Cavalry Regiment, and was assigned the rank of colonel. He fought at the battle of Shiloh and was taken prisoner shortly thereafter by the Confederate General Nathan Bedford Forrest, who would later help found the Ku Klux Klan. In an arrangement that seems positively quaint after the total warfare of the past century, Ingersoll was paroled on nothing grander than a promise to go home and fight no more.

Waiting for him back in Illinois was Eva Parker, now Ingersoll, whom he had married on February 13, 1862, nine days before marching off to battle. It was a blissfully happy union, one that ended only with his death thirty-seven years later. Steady, loving Eva provided unshakable emotional support, and Ingersoll dedicated his first book, *The Gods and Other Lectures*, to her, calling her "a woman without superstition."

Indeed, as Orvin Larson observed in *American Infidel: Robert G. Ingersoll*, the best biography to date: "Eva Parker was a rationalist. Never caught in the coils of sin-and-hell, her approach to religious questions was emotionally uncomplicated. If she thought of God at all, it was, as a Deist might, of a remote, impersonal force. She could not take seriously the idea of a God made in the image of man, which was the only God her husband could take seriously, either in acceptance or in attack. Agnosticism came easy for her, it came hard for him."

Ingersoll never experienced the serene happiness and sense of sustaining purpose that faith can inspire in believers; it simply wasn't in his nature. Nor could he leave it alone. He knew the Bible better than most preachers, but, for him, from a very early age, religion was all snare and delusion — an affront to reason, a divider of humanity, something to combat with every bit of strength at one's disposal. Today, with our keen sensitivity to identity politics of all stripe, it would be easy to identify and extract passages from Ingersoll that would seem to convict him as a bigot. His writings thunder against Judaism, Catholicism, Protestantism, and (rather less fervently, for practitioners were uncommon in nineteenth-century America) Buddhism, Hinduism, and Islam, as well.

Still, the very breadth of Ingersoll's antipathy toward religious doctrines ought to exempt him from the charge of belaboring one above another;

moreover, he was usually considerate enough to channel his attacks not on subscribers to a creed but to the creed itself. Indeed, he was close to a number of his day's leading clergymen (including Henry Ward Beecher), and his heartfelt farewell to Reverend Alexander Clark is included in this volume.

A faithful husband, a devoted friend, a kindly father, a "soft touch" for those in need, a man keenly concerned with social issues — in many ways, Ingersoll embodied what the religious right has claimed as "Christian values." One of his latter-day champions and editors, Roger E. Greeley (himself a retired Unitarian minister), has gone so far as to call Ingersoll a "deeply religious man," although he adds some immediate and necessary qualifications: "If religion consists of living an honest, useful and loving life and seeking to add to our knowledge of ourselves and planet earth, then Robert Ingersoll was a deeply religious man. If, instead, it is believed that religion is the guarantee of a next-life for those who have memorized the proper passwords, Ingersoll is not, by these narrow standards, religious."

It was the doctrine of eternal punishment that Ingersoll hated most profoundly; he called it the "infamy of infamies" and denounced it in his work hundreds of times. "In the New Testament, death is not the end, but the beginning of punishment that has no end," he wrote. "In the Old Testament, when God had a man dead, he let him alone. But in the New Testament the trouble commences at death." And, on another occasion:

> I would not for anything blot out the faintest star that shines in the horizon of human despair, nor in the sky of human hope, but I will do what I can to get that infinite shadow out of the heart of man. . . . I would not for my life destroy one star of human hope but I want it so that when a poor woman rocks the cradle and sings a lullaby to the dimpled darling, she will not be compelled to believe that ninety-nine chances in one hundred she is raising kindling wood for hell.

Susan Jacoby, whose book *Freethinkers: A History of American Secularism* is an essential corrective to more traditional national narratives, observes that "Ingersoll's spotless reputation as a husband and father was a source of considerable frustration to those who would have loved to catch him in bed, dead or alive, with a young woman." His attitude toward women was unusual, she adds, in that "he combined a bedrock belief in the intellectual equality of the sexes with old-fashioned chivalry and idealization of romantic love."

This last is borne out repeatedly in Ingersoll's writing:

> If upon this earth we ever have a glimpse of heaven, it is when we pass a home in winter, at night, and through the windows, the curtains drawn aside, we see the family about the pleasant hearth; the old lady knitting; the cat playing with the yarn; the children wishing they had as many dolls or dollars or knives or somethings as there are sparks going out to join the roaring blast; the father reading and smoking, and the clouds rising like incense from the altar of domestic joy. I never passed such a house without feeling that I had received a benediction.

Jacoby starts her book by evoking what she clearly considers the high-water mark of nineteenth-century "freethought" — Ingersoll's 1876 oration delivered in Peoria on the centennial of the signing of the Declaration of Independence. "One hundred years ago, our fathers retired the gods from politics," Ingersoll began:

> Our fathers founded the first secular government that was ever founded in this world. The first secular government; the first government that said every church has exactly the same rights and no more; every religion has the same rights, and no more.
>
> You might as well have a government united by force with Art, or with Poetry, or with Oratory, as with Religion. Religion should have the influence upon mankind that its goodness, that its morality, its justice, its charity, its reason, and its argument give it, and no more. Religion should have the effect upon mankind that it necessarily has, and no more. The religion that has to be supported by law is not only without value, but a fraud and curse. The religious argument that has to be supported by a musket is hardly worth making. A prayer that must have a cannon behind it better never be uttered. Forgiveness ought not to go in partnership with shot and shell. Love need not carry knives and revolvers.

It was strong stuff — even 130 years later, one cannot imagine any traditional politician speaking such words and remaining in the game for very long.* By 1876 it had been obvious for some time that Ingersoll, for all of his passion, intelligence, and organizational abilities, could never be elected to higher office. After making a brilliant start — becoming the first attorney general of Illinois in 1867, while still in his early thirties, and then seeking (and nearly winning) the Republican nomination for governor the following year — he "came out" as an agnostic in an address commemorating the birth of Alexander von Humboldt, the German naturalist, on September 14, 1869:

> Slowly, beautifully, like the coming of the dawn, came the grand truth that the universe is governed by law — that disease fastens itself upon the good and upon the bad; that the tornado cannot be stopped by counting beads; that the rushing lava pauses not for bended knees, the lightning for clasped and uplifted hands, nor the cruel waves of the sea

* A 1999 Gallup poll indicated that less than half of the American public would support an acknowledged atheist for president under any circumstances.

for prayer; that paying tithes causes rather than prevents famine; that pleasure is not sin; that happiness is the only good; that demons and gods exist only in the imagination; that faith is a lullaby, sung to put the soul to sleep; that devotion is a bribe that fear offers to supposed power; that offering rewards in another world for obedience in this is simply buying a soul on credit; that knowledge consists in ascertaining the laws of nature, and that wisdom is the science of happiness.

From this there could be no turning back. Ingersoll would go on to give countless speeches for Republican causes and candidates (including the official nomination of "plumed knight" James G. Blaine for president at the 1876 national convention in Cincinnati), but his heretical views effectively ruled him out as a serious contender for public office.

Ingersoll spent the last quarter century of his life as a peripatetic, cheerful, Socratic gadfly, stinging fundamentalist America wherever and whenever he could. He loved the public eye, taking on any number of high-profile legal cases (many of them pro bono), giving countless wide-ranging interviews (few public figures in our history have been so constantly accessible to the press), and lecturing throughout the land. As Jacoby observed, "Ingersoll's audiences in the South, Middle West, and Far West received him not only as the leading voice of American freethought but as an emissary from cosmopolitan culture. His lectures drew on a combination of self-education and erudition, experience representing beleaguered small farmers in Peoria and major corporate and political clients in Washington and New York, early poverty and self-made wealth, rural roots and urban sophistication."

He died in the saddle, in the midst of writing a new essay and with a full schedule of engagements stretching ahead of him, in Dobbs Ferry, New York, on July 21, 1899, the death attributed to a heart attack. Inevitably, there were rumors that he had "recanted" on his deathbed. Nonsense, said Eva Parker Ingersoll: He "closed his eyes and passed away without a struggle, a pang or even a sigh." He was buried in Arlington National Cemetery.

The present volume is intended to whet curiosity about the life and work of a most unusual American for a generation and a country that still has need of him. It is, unapologetically, a reading edition for a present-day audience; I have cut his speeches silently and generously, placing an emphasis on subjects that seem to have a continuing relevance. Those who want unabridged Ingersoll can easily find him on-line (scanned onto the Web by selfless devotees) or in the "Dresden Edition" of his complete works. Copies of the latter volumes tend to be marked up and worn by years of use, as reliably tattered as secondhand copies of *The Joy of Cooking*. Their condition may serve as testament to the fact that the long-lost Colonel Ingersoll, our apostle of heterodoxy, was once read, and read seriously, that he freed a lot of minds, and may have it in him to free many more.

Tim Page
Baltimore, Maryland
February 2005

What's God Got to Do with It?

CENTENNIAL ORATION

— Peoria, Illinois, July 4, 1876 —

One hundred years ago, our fathers retired the gods from politics.

The Declaration of Independence is the grandest, the bravest, and the profoundest political document that was ever signed by the representatives of a people. It is the embodiment of physical and moral courage and of political wisdom.

I say of physical courage, because it was a declaration of war against the most powerful nation then on the globe; a declaration of war by thirteen weak, unorganized colonies; a declaration of war by a few people, without military stores, without wealth, without strength, against the most powerful kingdom on the earth; a declaration of war made when the British navy, at that day the mistress of every sea, was hovering along the coast of America, looking after defenseless towns and villages to ravage and destroy. It was made when thousands of English soldiers were upon our soil, and when the principal cities of America were in the substantial possession of the enemy. And so, I say, all things considered, it was the bravest political document ever signed by man. And if it was physically brave, the moral courage of the document is almost infinitely beyond the physical. They had the courage not only, but they had the almost infinite wisdom, to declare that all men are created equal.

With one blow, with one stroke of the pen, they struck down all the cruel, heartless barriers that aristocracy, that priest-craft, that king-craft had raised between man and man. They struck down with one immortal blow that infamous spirit of caste that makes a god almost a beast, and a beast almost a god. With one word, with one blow, they wiped away and utterly destroyed all that had been done by centuries of war — centuries of hypocrisy — centuries of injustice.

Our fathers founded the first secular government that was ever founded in this world. The first secular government; the first government that said every church has exactly the same rights and no more; every religion has the same rights, and no more. In other words, our fathers were the first men who had the sense, had the genius, to know that no church should be allowed to have a sword; that it should be allowed only to exert its moral influence.

You might as well have a government united by

force with Art, or with Poetry, or with Oratory, as with Religion. Religion should have the influence upon mankind that its goodness, that its morality, its justice, its charity, its reason, and its argument give it, and no more. Religion should have the effect upon mankind that it necessarily has, and no more. The religion that has to be supported by law is not only without value, but a fraud and curse. The religious argument that has to be supported by a musket is hardly worth making. A prayer that must have a cannon behind it better never be uttered. Forgiveness ought not to go in partnership with shot and shell. Love need not carry knives and revolvers.

They signed that Declaration of Independence, although they knew that it would produce a long, terrible, and bloody war. They looked forward and saw poverty, deprivation, gloom, and death. But they also saw, on the wrecked clouds of war, the beautiful bow of freedom.

I will not name any of the grand men who fought for liberty. All should be named, or none. I feel that the unknown soldier who was shot down without even his name being remembered — who was included only in a report of "a hundred killed," or "a hundred missing," nobody knowing even the number that attached to his august corpse — is entitled to as deep and heartfelt thanks as the titled leader who fell at the head of the host.

Our country is founded upon the dignity of labor — upon the equality of man. Ours is the first real Republic in the history of the world. Beneath our flag the people are free. We have retired the gods from politics. We have found that man is the only source of political power, and that the governed should govern. We have disfranchised the aristocrats of the air and have given one country to mankind.

GOD IN THE CONSTITUTION

— *1890* —

In this country it is admitted that the power to govern resides in the people themselves; that they are the only rightful source of authority.

For many centuries before the formation of our Government, before the promulgation of the Declaration of Independence, the people had but little voice in the affairs of nations. The source of authority was not in this world; kings were not crowned by their subjects, and the sceptre was not held by the consent of the governed. The king sat on his throne by the will of God, and for that reason was not accountable to the people for the exercise of his power. He commanded, and the people obeyed. He was lord of their bodies, and his partner, the priest, was lord of their souls. The government of earth was patterned after the kingdom on high. God was a supreme autocrat in heaven, whose will was law, and the king was a supreme autocrat on earth whose will was law. The God in heaven had inferior beings to do his will, and the king on earth had certain favorites and officers to do his. These officers were accountable to him, and he was responsible to God.

The Feudal system was supposed to be in accordance with the divine plan. The people were not governed by intelligence, but by threats and promises, by rewards and punishments. No effort was made to enlighten the common people; no one thought of educating a peasant — of developing the mind of a laborer. The people were created to support thrones and altars. Their destiny was to toil and obey — to work and want. They were to be satisfied with huts and hovels, with ignorance and rags, and their children must expect no more. In the presence of the king they fell upon their knees, and before the priest they groveled in the very dust. The poor peasant divided his earnings with the state, because he imagined it protected his body; he divided his crust with the church, believing that it protected his soul. He was the prey of Throne and Altar — one deformed his body, the other his mind — and these two vultures fed upon his toil. He was taught by the king to hate the people of other nations, and by the priest to despise the believers in all other religions. He was made the enemy of all people except his own. He had no sympathy with the peasants of other lands, enslaved and plundered like himself. He was kept in ignorance, because education is the enemy of superstition, and because education is the foe of that egotism often mistaken for patriotism.

The intelligent and good man holds in his affections the good and true of every land — the boundaries of countries are not the limitations of his sympathies. Caring nothing for race, or color, he loves those who speak other languages and worship other gods. Between him and those who suffer, there is no impassable gulf. He salutes the world, and extends the hand of friendship to the human race. He does not bow before a provincial and patriotic god — one who protects his tribe or nation, and abhors the rest of mankind.

Through all the ages of superstition, each nation has insisted that it was the peculiar care of the true God, and that it alone had the true religion — that the gods of other nations were false and fraudulent, and that other religions were wicked, ignorant and absurd. In this way the seeds of hatred had been sown, and in this way have been kindled the flames of war. Men have had no sympathy with those of a different complexion, with those who knelt at other altars and expressed their thoughts in other words — and even a difference in garments placed them beyond the sympathy of others. Every peculiarity was the food of prejudice and the excuse for hatred.

The boundaries of nations were at last crossed by commerce. People became somewhat acquainted, and they found that the virtues and vices were quite evenly distributed. At last, subjects became somewhat acquainted with kings — peasants had the pleasure of gazing at princes, and it was dimly perceived that the differences were mostly in rags and names.

In 1776 our fathers endeavored to retire the gods from politics. They declared that "all governments derive their just powers from the consent of the governed." This was a contradiction of the then political ideas of the world; it was, as many believed, an act of pure blasphemy — a renunciation of the Deity. It was in fact a declaration of the independence of the earth. It was a notice to all churches and priests that thereafter mankind would govern and protect themselves. Politically it tore down every altar and denied the authority of every "sacred book," and appealed from the Providence of God to the Providence of Man. Those who promulgated the Declaration adopted a Constitution for the great Republic.

What was the office or purpose of that Constitution? Admitting that all power came from the people, it was necessary, first, that certain means be adopted for the purpose of ascertaining the will of the people, and second, it was proper and convenient to designate certain departments that should exercise certain powers of the Government. There must be the legislative, the judicial and the executive departments. Those who make laws should not execute them. Those who execute laws should not have the power of absolutely determining their meaning or their constitutionality. For these reasons, among others, a Constitution was adopted.

This Constitution also contained a declaration of rights. It marked out the limitations of discretion, so that in the excitement of passion, men shall not go beyond the point designated in the calm moment of reason. When man is unprejudiced, and his passions subject to reason, it is well he should define the limits of power, so that the waves driven by the storm of passion shall not overbear the shore.

A constitution is the chain the people put upon their servants, as well as upon themselves. It defines the limit of power and the limit of obedience. It follows, then, that nothing should be in a constitution that cannot be enforced by the power of the state. Behind every provision of the Constitution should stand the force of the nation.

Suppose, then, that we amend the Constitution and acknowledge the existence and supremacy of God — what becomes of the supremacy of the people, and how is this amendment to be enforced? A constitution does not enforce itself. It must be carried out by appropriate legislation.

Will it be a crime to deny the existence of this constitutional God? Can the offender be proceeded against in the criminal courts? Can his lips be closed by the power of the state? Would not this be the inauguration of religious persecution?

And if there is to be an acknowledgment of God in the Constitution, the question naturally arises as to which God is to have this honor. Shall we select the God of the Catholics — he who has established an infallible church presided over by an infallible pope, and who is delighted with certain ceremonies and placated by prayers uttered in exceedingly common Latin? Is it the God of the Presbyterian with the Five Points of Calvinism, who is ingenious enough to harmonize necessity and responsibility, and who in some way justifies himself for damning most of his own children? Is it the God of the Puritan, the enemy of joy — of the Baptist, who is great enough to govern the universe, and small enough to allow the destiny of a soul to depend on whether the body it inhabited was immersed or sprinkled? What God is it proposed to put in the Constitution? Is it the God of the Old Testament, who was a believer in slavery and who justified polygamy? If slavery was right then, it is right now; and if Jehovah was right then, the Mormons are right now. Are we to have the God who issued a commandment against all art — who was the enemy of investigation and of free speech? Is it the God who commanded the husband to stone his wife to death because she differed with him on the subject of religion? Are we to have a God who will re-enact the Mosaic code and punish hundreds of offences with death? What court, what tribunal of last resort, is to define this God, and who is to make known his will? In his presence, laws passed by men will be of no value. The decisions of courts will be as nothing. But who is to make known the will of this supreme God? Will there be a supreme tribunal composed of priests?

Of course all persons elected to office will either swear or affirm to support the Constitution. Men who do not believe in this God cannot so swear or affirm. Such men will not be allowed to hold any office of trust or honor. A God in the Constitution will not interfere with the oaths or affirmations of hypocrites. Such a provision will only exclude honest and conscientious unbelievers. Intelligent people know that no one knows whether there is a God or not. The existence of such a Being is merely a matter of opinion.

Men who believe in the liberty of man, who are willing to die for the honor of their country, will be excluded from taking any part in the administration of its affairs. Such a provision would place the country under the feet of priests. To recognize a Deity in the organic law of our country would be the destruction of religious liberty. The God in the Constitution would have to be protected. There would be laws against blasphemy, laws against the publication of honest thoughts, laws against carrying books and papers in the mails in which this constitutional God should be attacked. Our land would be filled with theological spies, with religious eavesdroppers, and all the snakes and reptiles of the lowest natures, in this sunshine of religious authority, would uncoil and crawl.

It is proposed to acknowledge a God who is the lawful and rightful Governor of nations; the one who ordained the powers that be. If this God is really the Governor of nations, it is not necessary to acknowledge him in the Constitution. This would not add to his power. If he governs all nations now, he has always controlled the affairs of men.

Having this control, why did he not see to it that he was recognized in the Constitution of the United States? If he had the supreme authority and neglected to put himself in the Constitution, is not this, at least, *prima facie* evidence that he did not desire to be there? For one, I am not in favor of the God who has "ordained the powers that be." What have we to say of Russia — of Siberia? What can we say of the persecuted and enslaved? What of the kings and nobles who live on the stolen labor of others? What of the priest and cardinal and pope who wrest, even from the hand of poverty, the single coin thrice earned? Is it possible to flatter the Infinite with a constitutional amendment? The Confederate States acknowledged God in their constitution, and yet they were overwhelmed by a people in whose organic law no reference to God is made. All the kings of the earth acknowledge the existence of God, and God is their ally; and this belief in God is used as a means to enslave and rob, to govern and degrade the people whom they call their subjects.

The Government of the United States is secular. It derives its power from the consent of man.

It is a Government with which God has nothing whatever to do — and all forms and customs, inconsistent with the fundamental fact that the people are the source of authority, should be abandoned. In this country there should be no oaths — no man should be sworn to tell the truth, and in no court should there be any appeal to any supreme being. A rascal by taking the oath appears to go in partnership with God, and ignorant jurors credit the firm instead of the man. A witness should tell his story, and if he speaks falsely should be considered as guilty of perjury. Governors and Presidents should not issue religious proclamations. They should not call upon the people to thank God. It is no part of their official duty. It is outside of and beyond the horizon of their authority. There is nothing in the Constitution of the United States to justify this religious impertinence.

For many years priests have attempted to give to our Government a religious form. Zealots have succeeded in putting the legend upon our money: "In God We Trust"; and we have chaplains in the army and navy, and legislative proceedings are usually opened with prayer. All this is contrary to the genius of the Republic, contrary to the Declaration of Independence, and contrary really to the

Constitution of the United States. We have taken the ground that the people can govern themselves without the assistance of any supernatural power. We have taken the position that the people are the real and only rightful source of authority. We have solemnly declared that the people must determine what is politically right and what is wrong, and that their legally expressed will is the supreme law. This leaves no room for national superstition — no room for patriotic gods or supernatural beings — and this does away with the necessity for political prayers.

The government of God has been tried. It was tried in Palestine several thousand years ago, and the God of the Jews was a monster of cruelty and ignorance, and the people governed by this God lost their nationality. Theocracy was tried through the Middle Ages. God was the Governor — the pope was his agent, and every priest and bishop and cardinal was armed with credentials from the Most High — and the result was that the noblest and best were in prisons, the greatest and grandest perished at the stake. The result was that vices were crowned with honor, and virtues whipped naked through the streets. The result was that hypocrisy swayed the sceptre of authority, while honesty languished in the dungeons of the Inquisition.

The result was that investigation was a crime, and the expression of an honest thought a capital offence. This government of God was established in Spain, and the Jews were expelled, the Moors were driven out, Moriscoes were exterminated, and nothing left but the ignorant and bankrupt worshipers of this monster. This government of God was tried in the United States when slavery was regarded as a divine institution, when men and women were regarded as criminals because they sought for liberty by flight, and when others were regarded as criminals because they gave them food and shelter. The pulpit of that day defended the buying and selling of women and babes, and the mouths of slave-traders were filled with passages of Scripture, defending and upholding the traffic in human flesh.

We have entered upon a new epoch. This is the century of man. Every effort to really better the condition of mankind has been opposed by the worshipers of some God. The church in all ages and among all peoples has been the consistent enemy of the human race. Everywhere and at all times, it has opposed the liberty of thought and expression. It has been the sworn enemy of investigation and of intellectual development. It has denied the existence of facts, the tendency of which was to undermine its power. It has always been carrying fagots to the feet of Philosophy. It has erected the gallows for Genius. It has built the dungeon for Thinkers. And today the orthodox church is as much opposed as it ever was to the mental freedom of the human race. Of course, there is a distinction made between churches and individual members. There have been millions of Christians who have been believers in liberty and in the freedom of expression — millions who have fought for the rights of man — but churches as organizations, have been on the other side. It is true that churches have fought churches — that Protestants battled with the Catholics for what they were pleased to call the freedom of conscience; and it is also true that the moment these Protestants obtained the civil power, they denied this freedom of conscience to others.

If God is allowed in the Constitution, man must abdicate. There is no room for both. If the people of the great Republic become superstitious enough and ignorant enough to put God in the Constitution of the United States, the experiment of self-government will have failed, and the great and splendid declaration that "all governments derive their just powers from the consent of the governed" will have been denied, and in its place will be found this: All power comes from God; priests are his agents, the people are their slaves.

Religion is an individual matter, and each soul should be left entirely free to form its own opinions and to judge of its accountability to a supposed supreme being. With religion, government has nothing whatever to do. Government is founded upon force, and force should never interfere with the religious opinions of men. Laws should define the rights of men and their duties toward each other, and these laws should be for the benefit of man in this world.

A nation can neither be Christian nor Infidel — a nation is incapable of having opinions upon these subjects. If a nation is Christian, will all the citizens go to heaven? If it is not, will they all be damned? Of course it is admitted that the majority of citizens composing a nation may believe or disbelieve, and they may call the nation what they please. A nation is a corporation. To repeat a familiar saying, "it has no soul." There can be no such thing as a Christian corporation. Several Christians may form a corporation, but it can hardly be said that the corporation thus formed was included in the atonement. For instance: Seven Christians form a corporation — that is to say, there are seven natural persons and one artificial — can it be said that there are eight souls to be saved?

No human being has brain enough, or knowledge enough, or experience enough, to say whether there is, or is not, a God. Into this darkness Science has not yet carried its torch. No human being has gone beyond the horizon of the natural. As to the existence of the supernatural, one man knows precisely as much, and exactly as little as another. Upon this question, chimpanzees and cardinals, apes and popes, are upon exact equality. The smallest insect discernible only by the most powerful microscope is as familiar with this subject as the greatest genius that has been produced by the human race. Governments and laws are for the preservation of rights and the regulation of conduct. One man should not be allowed to interfere with the liberty of another. In the metaphysical world there should be no interference whatever. The same is true in the world of art. Laws cannot regulate what is or is not music, what is or what is not beautiful — and constitutions cannot definitely settle and determine the perfection of statues, the value of paintings, or the glory and subtlety of thought. In spite of laws and constitutions the brain will think. In every direction consistent with the well-being and peace of society, there should be freedom. No man should be compelled to adopt the theology of another; neither should a minority, however small, be forced to acquiesce in the opinions of a majority, however large.

If there be an infinite Being, he does not need our help — we need not waste our energies in his defense. It is enough for us to give to every other human being the liberty we claim for ourselves. There may or may not be a Supreme Ruler of the universe — but we are certain that man exists, and we believe that freedom is the condition of progress; that it is the sunshine of the mental and moral world, and that without it man will go back to the den of savagery, and will become the fit associate of wild and ferocious beasts.

We have tried the government of priests, and we know that such governments are without mercy. In the administration of theocracy, all the instruments of torture have been invented. If any man wishes to have God recognized in the Constitution of our country, let him read the history of the Inquisition, and let him remember that hundreds of millions of men, women and children have been sacrificed to placate the wrath, or win the approbation of this God.

There has been in our country a divorce of church and state. This follows as a natural sequence of the declaration that "governments derive their just powers from the consent of the governed." The priest was no longer a necessity. His presence was a contradiction of the principle on which the Republic was founded. He represented, not the authority of the people, but of some "Power from on High," and to recognize this other Power was inconsistent with free government. The founders of the Republic at that time parted company with the priests, and said to them: "You may turn your attention to the other world — we will attend to the affairs of this." Equal liberty was given to all. But the ultra-theologian is not satisfied with this — he wishes to destroy the liberty of the people — he wishes a recognition of his God as the source of authority, to the end that the church may become the supreme power. But the sun will not be turned backward. The people of the United States are intelligent. They no longer believe implicitly in supernatural religion. They are losing confidence in the miracles and marvels of the Dark Ages. They know the value of the free school. They appreciate the benefits of science. They are believers in education, in the free play of thought, and there is a suspicion that the priest, the theologian, is destined to take his place with the necromancer, the astrologer, the worker of magic, and the professor of the black art.

We have already compared the benefits of theology and science. When the theologian governed the world, it was covered with huts and hovels for the many, palaces and cathedrals for the few. To nearly all the children of men, reading and writing were unknown arts. The poor were clad in rags and skins — they devoured crusts, and gnawed bones. The day of Science dawned, and the luxuries of a century ago are the necessities of today. Men in the middle ranks of life have more of the conveniences and elegancies than the princes and kings of the theological times. But above and over all this is the development of mind. There is more of value in the brain of an average man of today — of a master-mechanic, of a chemist, of a naturalist, of an inventor, than there was in the brain of the world four hundred years ago.

These blessings did not fall from the skies. These benefits did not drop from the outstretched hands of priests. They were not found in cathedrals or behind altars — neither were they searched for with holy candles. They were not discovered by the closed eyes of prayer, nor did they come in answer to superstitious supplication. They are the children of freedom, the gifts of reason, observation and experience — and for them all, man is indebted to man.

Let us hold fast to the sublime declaration of Lincoln. Let us insist that this, the Republic, is "a government of the people, by the people, and for the people."

A CHRISTMAS SERMON

— *1891* —

The good part of Christmas is not always Christian — it is generally Pagan; that is to say, human, natural.

Long before Christ was born the Sun-God triumphed over the powers of Darkness. About the time that we call Christmas the days begin perceptibly to lengthen. Our barbarian ancestors were worshipers of the sun, and they celebrated his victory over the hosts of night. Such a festival was natural and beautiful. The most natural of all religions is the worship of the sun. Christianity adopted this festival. It borrowed from the Pagans the best it has.

I believe in Christmas and in every day that has been set apart for joy. We in America have too much work and not enough play. We are too much like the English.

I think it was Heinrich Heine who said that he thought a blaspheming Frenchman was a more pleasing object to God than a praying Englishman. We take our joys too sadly. I am in favor of all the good free days — the more the better.

Christmas is a good day to forgive and forget — a good day to throw away prejudices and hatreds — a good day to fill your heart and your house, and the hearts and houses of others, with sunshine.

THE LIBERTY OF MAN,
WOMAN AND CHILD

— *1877* —

What do I mean by liberty? By physical liberty I mean the right to do anything which does not interfere with the happiness of another. By intellectual liberty I mean the right to think right and the right to think wrong. Thought is the means by which we endeavor to arrive at truth. If we know the truth already, we need not think. All that can be required is honesty of purpose. You ask my opinion about anything; I examine it honestly, and when my mind is made up, what should I tell you? Should I tell you my real thought? What should I do? There is a book put in my hands. I am told this is the Koran; it was written by inspiration. I read it, and when I get through, suppose that I think in my heart and in my brain, that it is utterly untrue, and you then ask me, what do you think? Now, admitting that I live in Turkey, and have no chance to get any office unless I am on the side of the Koran, what should I say? Should I make a clean breast and say, that upon my honor I do not believe it? What would you think then of my fellow-citizens if they said: "That man is dangerous, he is dishonest."

Suppose I read the book called the Bible, and when I get through I make up my mind that it was written by men. A minister asks me, "Did you read the Bible?" I answer that I did. "Do you think it divinely inspired?" What should I reply? Should I say to myself, "If I deny the inspiration of the Scriptures, the people will never clothe me with power." What ought I to answer? Ought I not to say like a man: "I have read it; I do not believe it." Should I not give the real transcript of my mind? Or should I turn hypocrite and pretend what I do not feel, and hate myself forever after for being a cringing coward. For my part I would rather a man would tell me what he honestly thinks. I would rather he would preserve his manhood. I had a thousand times rather be a manly unbeliever than an unmanly believer. And if there is a Judgment Day, a time when all will stand before some Supreme Being, I believe I will stand higher, and stand a better chance of getting my case decided in my favor, than any man sneaking through life pretending to believe what he does not.

I read in a book that the Supreme Being concluded to make a world and one man; that he took some nothing and made a world and one man, and put this man in a garden. In a little while he noticed that the man got lonesome; that he wandered around as if he was waiting for a train. There was nothing to interest him; no news; no papers; no politics; no policy; and, as the devil had not yet made his appearance, there was no chance for reconciliation; not even for civil service reform. Well, he wandered about the garden in this condition, until finally the Supreme Being made up his mind to make him a companion.

Having used up all the nothing he originally took in making the world and one man, he had to take a part of the man to start a woman with. So he caused a sleep to fall on this man — now understand me, I do not say this story is true. After the sleep fell upon this man, the Supreme Being took a rib, or as the French would call it, a cutlet, out of this man, and from that he made a woman. And considering the amount of raw material used, I look upon it as the most successful job ever performed. Well, after he got the woman done, she was brought to the man; not to see how she liked him, but to see how he liked her. He liked her, and they started housekeeping; and they were told of certain things they might do and of one thing they could not do — and of course they did it. I would have done it in fifteen minutes, and I know it. And then they were turned out of the park and extra policemen were put on to keep them from getting back in.

Devilment commenced. The mumps, and the measles, and the whooping-cough, and the scarlet fever started in their race for man. They began to have the toothache, roses began to have thorns, snakes began to have poisoned teeth, and people began to divide about religion and politics, and the world has been full of trouble from that day to this.

The Liberty of Women

In my judgment, the woman is the equal of the man. She has all the rights I have and one more, and that is the right to be protected. That is my doctrine. You are married; try and make the woman you love happy. Whoever marries simply for himself will make a mistake; but whoever loves a woman so well that he says, "I will make her happy," makes no mistake. And so with the woman who says, "I will make him happy." There is only one way to be happy, and that is to make somebody else so, and you cannot be happy by going cross lots; you have got to go the regular turnpike road.

If there is any man I detest, it is the man who thinks he is the head of a family.

Imagine a young man and a young woman courting, walking out in the moonlight, and the nightingale singing a song of pain and love, as though the thorn touched her heart — imagine them stopping there in the moonlight and starlight and song, and saying, "Now, here, let us settle who is boss!" I tell you it is an infamous word and an infamous feeling — I abhor a man who is "boss," who is going to govern in his family, and when he speaks orders all the rest are to be still as some mighty idea is about to be launched from his mouth. Do you know I dislike this man unspeakably?

I hate above all things a cross man. What right has he to murder the sunshine of a day? What right has he to assassinate the Joy of life? When you go home you ought to go like a ray of light — so that it will, even in the night, burst out of the doors and windows and illuminate the darkness. Some men think their mighty brains have been in a turmoil; they have been thinking about who will be alderman from the fifth ward; they have been thinking about politics; great and mighty questions have been engaging their minds; they have bought calico at five cents or six, and want to sell it for seven. Think of the intellectual strain that must have been upon that man, and when he gets home everybody else in the house must look out for his comfort. A woman who has only taken care of five or six children, and one or two of them sick, has been nursing them and singing to them, and trying to make one yard of cloth do the work of two, she, of course, is fresh and fine and ready to wait upon this gentleman — the head of the family — the boss!

Get the best you can for your family — try to look as well as you can yourself. When you used to go courting, how elegantly you looked! Ah, your eye was bright, your sleep was light, and you looked like a prince. Do you know that it is insufferable egotism in you to suppose a woman is going to love you always looking as slovenly as you can? Think of it! Any good woman on earth will be true to you forever when you do your level best.

Some people tell me, "Your doctrine about loving, and wives, and all that, is splendid for the rich, but it won't do for the poor." I tell you tonight there is more love in the homes of the poor than in the palaces of the rich. The meanest hut with love in it is a palace fit for the gods, and a palace without love is a den only fit for wild beasts. That is my doctrine!

You cannot be so poor that you cannot help somebody. Good nature is the cheapest commodity in the world; and love is the only thing that will pay ten per cent to borrower and lender both. Do not tell me that you have got to be rich! We have a false standard of greatness in the United States. We think here that a man must be great, that he must be notorious; that he must be extremely wealthy, or that his name must be upon the putrid lips of rumor. It is all a mistake. It is not necessary to be rich or to be great, or to be powerful, to be happy. The happy man is the successful man.

Happiness is the legal tender of the soul.

Joy is wealth.

The Liberty of Children

If women have been slaves, what shall I say of children; of the little children in alleys and sub-cellars; the little children who turn pale when they hear their father's footsteps; little children who run away when they only hear their names called by the lips of a mother; little children — the children of poverty, the children of crime, the children of brutality, wherever they are — flotsam and jetsam upon the wild, mad sea of life — my heart goes out to them, one and all.

When your little child tells a lie, do not rush at him as though the world were about to go into bankruptcy. Be honest with him. A tyrant father will have liars for his children; do you know that? A lie is born of tyranny upon the one hand and weakness upon the other, and when you rush at a poor little boy with a club in your hand, of course he lies.

I thank thee, Mother Nature, that thou hast put ingenuity enough in the brain of a child, when attacked by a brutal parent, to throw up a little breastwork in the shape of a lie.

When one of your children tells a lie, be honest with him; tell him that you have told hundreds of them yourself. Tell him it is not the best way; that you have tried it. Tell him as the man did in Maine when his boy left home: "John, honesty is the best policy; I have tried both." Be honest with him. Suppose a man as much larger than you as you are larger than a child five years old, should come at you with a liberty pole in his hand, and in a voice of thunder shout, "Who broke that plate?" There is not a solitary one of you who would not swear you never saw it, or that it was cracked when you got it. Why not be honest with these children? Just imagine a man who deals in stocks whipping his boy for putting false rumors afloat! Think of a lawyer beating his own flesh and blood for evading the truth when he makes half of his own living that way! Think of a minister punishing his child for not telling all he thinks!

When your child commits a wrong, take it in your arms; let it feel your heart beat against its heart; let the child know that you really and truly and sincerely love it. Yet some Christians, good Christians, when a child commits a fault, drive it from the door and say: "Never do you darken this house again." And then these same people will get down on their knees and ask God to take care of the child they have driven from home. I will never ask God to take care of my children unless I am doing my level best in that same direction.

But I will tell you what I say to my children: "Go where you will; commit what crime you may; fall to what depth of degradation you may; you can never commit any crime that will shut my door, my arms, or my heart to you. As long as I live you shall have one sincere friend."

I do not believe in the government of the lash. If any one of you ever expects to whip your children again, I want you to have a photograph taken of yourself when you are in the act, with your face red with vulgar anger, and the face of the little child, with eyes swimming in tears and the little chin dimpled with fear, like a piece of water struck by a sudden cold wind. Have the picture taken. If that little child should die, I cannot think of a sweeter way to spend an autumn afternoon than to go out to the cemetery, when the maples are clad in tender gold, and little scarlet runners are coming, like poems of regret, from the sad heart of the earth — and sit down upon the grave and look at that photograph, and think of the flesh now dust that you beat. I tell you it is wrong; it is no way to raise children! Make your home happy. Be honest with them. Divide fairly with them in everything.

I intend so to treat my children, that they can come to my grave and truthfully say: "He who sleeps here never gave us a moment of pain. From his lips, now dust, never came to us an unkind word."

In the olden time, they thought some days were too good for a child to enjoy himself. When I was a boy Sunday was considered altogether too holy to be happy in. Sunday used to commence then when the sun went down on Saturday night. We commenced at that time for the purpose of getting a good ready, and when the sun fell below the horizon on Saturday evening, there was a darkness fell upon the house ten thousand times deeper than that of night. Nobody said a pleasant word; nobody laughed; nobody smiled; the child that looked the sickest was regarded as the most pious. That night you could not even crack hickory nuts. If you were caught chewing gum it was only another evidence of the total depravity of the human heart. It was an exceedingly solemn night. Dyspepsia was in the very air you breathed. Everybody looked sad and mournful. I have noticed all my life that many people think they have religion when they are troubled with dyspepsia. If there could be found an absolute specific for that disease, it would be the hardest blow the church has ever received.

On Sunday morning the solemnity had simply increased. Then we went to church. The minister was in a pulpit about twenty feet high, with a little sounding-board above him, and he commenced at "firstly" and went on and on and on to about "twenty-thirdly." Then he made a few remarks by way of application; and then took a general view of the subject, and in about two hours reached the last chapter in Revelation.

After the sermon we had an intermission. Then came the catechism with the chief end of man. We went through with that. We sat in a row with our feet coming in about six inches off the floor. The minister asked us if we knew that we all deserved to go to hell, and we all answered "Yes." Then we were asked if we would be willing to go to hell if it was God's will, and every little liar shouted "Yes." Then the same sermon was preached once more, commencing at the other end and going back. After that, we started for home, sad and solemn — overpowered with the wisdom displayed in the scheme of the atonement. When we got home, if we had been good boys, and the weather was warm, sometimes they would take us out to the graveyard to cheer us up a little. It did cheer me. When I looked at the sunken tombs and the leaning stones, and read the half-effaced inscriptions through the moss of silence and forgetfulness, it was a great comfort. The reflection came to my mind that the observance of the Sabbath could not last always. Sometimes they would sing that beautiful hymn in which occurs these cheerful lines:

> *Where congregations never break up*
> *And Sabbaths never end.*

These lines, I think, prejudiced me a little against even heaven.

Sabbaths used to be prisons. Every Sunday was a Bastille. Every Christian was a kind of turnkey, and every child was a prisoner — a convict. In that dungeon, a smile was a crime.

As long as men and women are afraid of the church, as long as a minister inspires fear, as long as people reverence a thing simply because they do not understand it, as long as it is respectable to lose your self-respect, as long as the church has power, as long as mankind worships a book, just so long will the world be filled with intellectual paupers and vagrants, covered with the soiled and faded rags of superstition.

As long as woman regards the Bible as the charter of her rights, she will be the slave of man. The Bible was not written by a woman. Within its lids there is nothing but humiliation and shame for her. She is regarded as the property of man. She is made to ask forgiveness for becoming a mother. She is as much below her husband as her husband is below Christ. She is not allowed to speak. The gospel is too pure to be spoken by her polluted lips. Woman should learn in silence.

In the Bible will be found no description of a civilized home. The free mother surrounded by free and loving children, adored by a free man, her husband, was unknown to the inspired writers of the Bible. They did not believe in the democracy of home — in the republicanism of the fireside.

These inspired gentlemen knew nothing of the rights of children. They were the advocates of brute force — the disciples of the lash. They knew nothing of human rights. Their doctrines have brutalized the homes of millions, and filled the eyes of infancy with tears.

There has never been upon the earth a generation of free men and women. It is not yet time to write a creed. Wait until the chains are broken — until dungeons are not regarded as temples. Wait until solemnity is not mistaken for wisdom — until mental cowardice ceases to be known as reverence. Wait until the living are considered the equals of the dead — until the cradle takes precedence of the coffin. Wait until what we know can be spoken without regard to what others may believe. Wait until teachers take the place of preachers — until followers become investigators. Wait until the world is free before you write a creed.

In this creed there will be but one word — Liberty.

ON THE ACCOMPLISHMENTS
OF FREETHOUGHT

— 1890 —

We have destroyed the idea that a monster created and governs this world — the declaration that a God of infinite mercy and compassion upheld slavery and polygamy and commanded the destruction of men, women, and babes. We have destroyed the idea that this monster created a few of his children for eternal joy, and the vast majority for everlasting pain. We have destroyed the infinite absurdity that salvation depends upon belief, that investigation is dangerous, and that the torch of reason lights only the way to hell. We have taken a grinning devil from every grave, and the curse from death — and in the place of these dogmas, of these infamies, we have put that which is natural and that which commends itself to the heart and brain.

Instead of loving God, we love each other. Instead of the religion of the sky — the religion of this world — the religion of the family — the love of husband for wife, of wife for husband — the love of all for children. So that now the real religion is: Let us live for each other; let us live for this world, without regard for the past and without fear for the future. Let us use our faculties and our powers for the benefit of ourselves and others, knowing that if there be another world, the same philosophy that gives us joy here will make us happy there.

Nothing can be more absurd than the idea that we can do something to please or displease an infinite Being. If our thoughts and actions can lessen or increase the happiness of God, then to that extent God is the slave and victim of man.

THOMAS PAINE
— 1877 —

In all ages reason has been regarded as the enemy of religion. Nothing has been considered so pleasing to the Deity as a total denial of the authority of your own mind. Self-reliance has been thought a deadly sin; and the idea of living and dying without the aid and consolation of superstition has always horrified the church. By some unaccountable infatuation, belief has been and still is considered of immense importance. All religions have been based upon the idea that God will forever reward the true believer, and eternally damn the man who doubts. Belief is regarded as the one essential thing. To practice justice, to love mercy, is not enough. You must believe in some incomprehensible creed. You must say, "Once one is three, and three times one is one." The man who practiced every virtue, but failed to believe, was execrated. Nothing so outrages the feelings of the church as a moral unbeliever — nothing so horrible as a charitable Atheist.

For the overthrow of this infamous tenet, Paine exerted all his strength. He left few arguments to be used by those who should come after him, and he used none that have been refuted. The combined wisdom and genius of all mankind cannot possibly conceive of an argument against liberty of thought. Neither can they show why any one should be punished, either in this world or another, for acting honestly in accordance with reason. And yet a doctrine with every possible argument against it has been, and still is, believed and defended by the entire orthodox world. Can it be possible that we have been endowed with reason simply that our souls may be caught in its toils and snares, that we may be led by its false and delusive glare out of the narrow path that leads to joy into the broad way of everlasting death? Is it possible that we have been given reason simply that we may through faith ignore its deductions, and avoid its conclusions? Ought the sailor to throw away his compass and depend entirely upon the fog? If reason is not to be depended upon in matters of religion, that is to say, in respect of our duties to the Deity, why should it be relied upon in matters respecting the rights of our fellows?

If a man should tell you that he had the most beautiful painting in the world, and after taking you where it was should insist upon having your eyes shut, you would likely suspect either that he had no painting or that it was some pitiable daub. Should he tell you that he was a most excellent performer on the violin, and yet refuse to play unless your ears were stopped, you would think, to say the least of it, that he had an odd way of convincing you of his musical ability. But would his conduct be any more wonderful than that of a religionist who asks that before examining his creed you will have the kindness to throw away your reason? The first gentleman says, "Keep your eyes shut, my picture will bear everything but being seen"; "Keep your ears stopped, my music objects to nothing but being heard." The last says, "Away with your reason, my religion dreads nothing but being understood."

The Christianity of Paine's day is not the Christianity of our time. There has been a great improvement since then. One hundred and fifty years ago the foremost preachers of our time would have perished at the stake. A Universalist would have been torn in pieces in England, Scotland, and America. Unitarians would have found themselves in the stocks, pelted by the rabble with dead cats, after which their ears would have been cut off, their tongues bored, and their foreheads branded. Less than one hundred and fifty years ago the following law was in force in Maryland:

> Be it enacted by the Right Honorable, the Lord Proprietor, by and with the device and consent of his Lordship's governor, and the upper and lower houses of the Assembly, and the authority of the same:
>
>> That if any person shall hereafter, within this province, wittingly, maliciously, and advisedly, by writing or speaking, blaspheme or curse God, or deny our Savior, Jesus Christ, to be the Son of God, or shall deny the Holy Trinity, the Father, Son, and Holy Ghost, or the Godhead of any of the three persons, or the unity of the Godhead, or shall utter any profane words concerning the Holy Trinity, or any of the persons thereof, and shall thereof be convicted by verdict, shall, for the last offence, be bored through the tongue, and fined twenty pounds to be levied of his body. And for the second offence, the offender shall be stigmatized by burning in the forehead

> with the letter B, and fined forty
> pounds. And that for the third offence
> the offender shall suffer death without
> the benefit of clergy.

The strange thing about this law is that it has never been repealed, and is still in force in the District of Columbia. Laws like this were in force in most of the colonies, and in all countries where the church had power.

Under such conditions progress was impossible. Someone had to lead the way. The church is, and always has been, incapable of a forward movement. Religion always looks back. The church has already reduced Spain to a guitar, Italy to a hand-organ, and Ireland to exile.

In our country the church was all-powerful, and although divided into many sects, would instantly unite to repel a common foe.

Paine struck the first grand blow.

The Age of Reason did more to undermine the power of the Protestant Church than all other books then known. It furnished an immense amount of food for thought. It was written for the average mind, and is a straightforward, honest investigation of the Bible, and of the Christian system.

Paine did not falter, from the first page to the last. He gives you his candid thought, and candid thoughts are always valuable.

The Age of Reason has liberalized us all. It put arguments in the mouths of the people; it put the church on the defensive; it enabled somebody in every village to corner the parson; it made the world wiser, and the church better; it took power from the pulpit and divided it among the pews.

Every church pretends to have found the exact truth. This is the end of progress. Why pursue that which you have? Why investigate when you know?

Every creed is a rock in running water: humanity sweeps by it. Every creed cries to the universe, "Halt!" A creed is the ignorant Past bullying the enlightened Present.

The ignorant are not satisfied with what can be demonstrated. Science is too slow for them, and so they invent creeds. They demand completeness. A sublime segment, a grand fragment, are of no value to them. They demand the complete circle — the entire structure.

In music they want a melody with a recurring accent at measured periods. In religion they insist upon immediate answers to the questions of creation and destiny. The alpha and omega of all things must be in the alphabet of their superstition. A religion that cannot answer every question, and guess every conundrum is, in their estimation, worse than worthless. They desire a kind of theological dictionary — a religious ready reckoner, together with guide-boards at all crossings and turns. They mistake impudence for authority, solemnity for wisdom, and bathos for inspiration. The beginning and the end are what they demand. The grand flight of the eagle is nothing to them. They want the nest in which he was hatched, and especially the dry limb upon which he roosts. Anything that can be learned is hardly worth knowing. The present is considered of no value in itself. Happiness must not be expected this side of the clouds, and can only be attained by self-denial and faith; not self-denial for the good of others, but for the salvation of your own sweet self.

Paine denied the authority of bibles and creeds; this was his crime, and for this the world shut the door in his face, and emptied its slops upon him from the windows.

I challenge the world to show that Thomas Paine ever wrote one line, one word in favor of tyranny — in favor of immorality; one line, one word against what he believed to be for the highest and best interest of mankind; one line, one word against justice, charity, or liberty, and yet he has been pursued as though he had been a fiend from hell.

The doubter, the investigator, the Infidel, have been the saviors of liberty. This truth is beginning to be realized, and the truly intellectual are honoring the brave thinkers of the past.

We need men with moral courage to speak and write their real thoughts, and to stand by their convictions, even to the very death. We need have no fear of being too radical. The future will verify all grand and brave predictions.

Thomas Paine was one of the intellectual heroes — one of the men to whom we are indebted. His name is associated forever with the Great Republic. As long as free government exists he will be remembered, admired and honored.

He lived a long, laborious and useful life. The world is better for his having lived. For the sake of truth he accepted hatred and reproach for his portion. He ate the bitter bread of sorrow. His friends were untrue to him because he was true to himself, and true to them. He lost the respect of what is called society, but kept his own. His life is what the world calls failure and what history calls success.

If to love your fellowmen more than self is goodness, Thomas Paine was good.

If to be in advance of your time — to be a pioneer in the direction of right — is greatness, Thomas Paine was great.

If to avow your principles and discharge your duty in the presence of death is heroic, Thomas Paine was a hero.

At the age of seventy-three, death touched his tired heart. He died in the land his genius defended — under the flag he gave to the skies. Slander cannot touch him now — hatred cannot reach him more. He sleeps in the sanctuary of the tomb, beneath the quiet of the stars.

A few more years — a few more brave men — a few more rays of light, and mankind will venerate the memory of him who said: "Any system of religion that shocks the mind of a child cannot be a true system," and "The world is my country, and to do good my religion."

ON LENT

— From an 1881 interview —

QUESTION

What have you to say about the attack of Dr. Buckley [a prominent Brooklyn churchman] on you, and your lecture?

ANSWER

I never heard of Dr. Buckley until after I had lectured in Brooklyn. He seems to think that it was extremely ill bred in me to deliver a lecture on the "Liberty of Man, Woman and Child" during Lent.

Lent is just as good as any other part of the year, and no part can be too good to do good. It was not a part of my object to hurt the feelings of the Episcopalians and Catholics. If they think that there is some subtle relation between hunger and heaven, or that faith depends upon, or is strengthened by famine, or that veal, during Lent, is the enemy of virtue, or that beef breeds blasphemy, while fish feeds faith — of course, all this is nothing to me. They have a right to say that vice depends on victuals, sanctity on soup, religion on rice and chastity on cheese, but they have no right to say that a lecture on liberty is an insult to them because they are hungry. I suppose that Lent was instituted in memory of the Savior's fast. At one time it was supposed that only a divine being could live forty days without food. This supposition has been overthrown.

What possible good did it do the world for Christ to go without food for forty days? Why should we follow such an example? As a rule, hungry people are cross, contrary, obstinate, peevish and unpleasant. A good dinner puts a man at peace with all the world — makes him generous, good natured and happy. He feels like kissing his wife and children. The future looks bright. He wants to help the needy. The good in him predominates, and he wonders that any man was ever stingy or cruel. Your good cook is a civilizer, and without good food, well prepared, intellectual progress is simply impossible. Most of the orthodox creeds were born of bad cooking. Bad food produced dyspepsia, and dyspepsia produced Calvinism, and Calvinism is the cancer of Christianity. Oatmeal is responsible for the worst features of Scotch Presbyterianism. Half cooked beans account for the religion of the Puritans. Fried bacon and saleratus biscuit underlie the doctrine of State Rights. Lent is a mistake, fasting is a blunder, and bad cooking is a crime.

ON REPUBLICANISM
— Wall Street speech, 1880 —

The city of New York owes a great debt to the country. Every man that has cleared a farm has helped to build New York; every man that helped to build a railway helped to build up the palaces of this city. Where I am now speaking are the termini of all the railways in the United States. They all come here. New York has been built up by the labor of the country, and New York owes it to the country to protect the best interests of the country.

I have a right to express my opinion, in common with every other human being, and I am willing to give to every other human being the right that I claim for myself. Republicanism means justice in politics. Republicanism means progress in civilization. Republicanism means that every man shall be an educated patriot and a gentleman. I want to say to you today that it is an honor to belong to the Republican party. It is an honor to have belonged to it for twenty years; it is an honor to belong to the party that elected Abraham Lincoln President. And let me say to you that Lincoln was the greatest, the best, the purest, the kindest man that has ever sat in the presidential chair. It is an honor to belong to the Republican party that gave four millions of men the rights of freemen; it is an honor to belong to the party that broke the shackles from four millions of men, women and children. It is an honor to belong to the party that declared that bloodhounds were not the missionaries of civilization. It is an honor to belong to the party that said it was a crime to steal a babe from its mother's breast. It is an honor to belong to the party that swore that this is a Nation forever, one and indivisible. It is an honor to belong to the party that elected U. S. Grant President of the United States. It is an honor to belong to the party that issued thousands and thousands of millions of dollars in promises — that issued promises until they became as thick as the withered leaves of winter; an honor to belong to the party that issued them to put down a rebellion; an honor to belong to the party that put it down; an honor to belong to the party that had the moral courage and honesty to make every one of the promises made in war, as good as shining, glittering gold in peace. And I tell you that if there is another life, and if there is a day of judgment, all you need say upon that solemn occasion is, "I was in life and in my death a good square Republican."

I belong to the party that is prosperous when the country is prosperous. I belong to the party that believes in good crops; that is glad when a fellow finds a gold mine; that rejoices when there are forty bushels of wheat to the acre; that laughs when every railroad declares dividends, that claps both its hands when every investment pays; when the rain falls for the farmer, when the dew lies lovingly on the grass. I belong to the party that is happy when the people are happy; when the laboring man gets three dollars a day; when he has roast beef on his table; when he has a carpet on the floor; when he has a picture of Garfield on the wall. I belong to the party that is happy when everybody smiles, when we have plenty of money, good horses, good carriages; when our wives are happy and our children feel glad. I belong to the party whose banner floats side by side with the great flag of the country; that does not grow fat on defeat.

ABRAHAM LINCOLN

— *1887* —

Abraham Lincoln was, in my judgment, in many respects, the grandest man ever President of the United States. Upon his monument these words should be written: "Here sleeps the only man in the history of the world who, having been clothed with almost absolute power, never abused it, except upon the side of mercy."

WHY I AM AN AGNOSTIC
— 1896 —

When I was a boy I heard them tell of an old farmer in Vermont. He was dying. The minister was at his bedside — asked him if he was a Christian — if he was prepared to die. The old man answered that he had made no preparation, that he was not a Christian — that he had never done anything but work. The preacher said that he could give him no hope unless he had faith in Christ, and that if he had no faith his soul would certainly be lost.

The old man was not frightened. He was perfectly calm. In a weak and broken voice he said: "Mr. Preacher, I suppose you noticed my farm. My wife and I came here more than fifty years ago. We were just married. It was a forest then and the land was covered with stones. I cut down the trees, burned the logs, picked up the stones and laid the walls. My wife spun and wove and worked every moment. We raised and educated our children — denied ourselves. During all these years my wife never had a good dress, or a decent bonnet. I never had a good suit of clothes. We lived on the plainest food. Our hands, our bodies are deformed by toil.

We never had a vacation. We loved each other and the children. That is the only luxury we ever had. Now I am about to die and you ask me if I am prepared. Mr. Preacher, I have no fear of the future, no terror of any other world. There may be such a place as hell — but if there is, you never can make me believe that it's any worse than old Vermont."

So, they told of a man who compared himself with his dog. "My dog," he said, "just barks and plays — has all he wants to eat. He never works — has no trouble about business. In a little while he dies, and that is all. I work with all my strength. I have no time to play. I have trouble every day. In a little while I will die, and then I go to hell. I wish that I had been a dog."

. . .

While the cold weather lasted, while the snows fell, the revival went on, but when the winter was over, when the steamboat's whistle was heard, when business started again, most of the converts "backslid" and fell again into their old ways. But the next winter they were on hand, ready to be "born again." They formed a kind of stock company, playing the same parts every winter and backsliding every spring.

The ministers, who preached at these revivals, were in earnest. They were zealous and sincere.

They were not philosophers. To them science was the name of a vague dread — a dangerous enemy. They did not know much, but they believed a great deal. To them hell was a burning reality — they could see the smoke and flames. The Devil was no myth. He was an actual person, a rival of God, an enemy of mankind. They thought that the important business of this life was to save your soul — that all should resist and scorn the pleasures of sense, and keep their eyes steadily fixed on the golden gate of the New Jerusalem. They were unbalanced, emotional, hysterical, bigoted, hateful, loving, and insane. They really believed the Bible to be the actual word of God — a book without mistake or contradiction. They called its cruelties, justice — its absurdities, mysteries — its miracles, facts, and the idiotic passages were regarded as profoundly spiritual. They dwelt on the pangs, the regrets, the infinite agonies of the lost, and showed how easily they could be avoided, and how cheaply heaven could be obtained. They told their hearers to believe, to have faith, to give their hearts to God, their sins to Christ, who would bear their burdens and make their souls as white as snow.

I heard hundreds of these evangelical sermons — heard hundreds of the most fearful and vivid descriptions of the tortures inflicted in hell, of the horrible state of the lost. I supposed that what I heard was true and yet I did not believe it. I said: "It is," and then I thought: "It cannot be."

These sermons made but faint impressions on my mind. I was not convinced. I had no desire to be "converted," did not want a "new heart" and had no wish to be "born again."

Having spent my youth in reading books about religion — about the "new birth" — the disobedience of our first parents, the atonement, salvation by faith, the wickedness of pleasure, the degrading consequences of love, and the impossibility of getting to heaven by being honest and generous, and having become somewhat weary of the frayed and raveled thoughts, you can imagine my surprise, my delight when I read the poems of Robert Burns.

I was familiar with the writings of the devout and insincere, the pious and petrified, the pure and heartless. Here was a natural honest man. I knew the works of those who regarded all nature as depraved, and looked upon love as the legacy and perpetual witness of original sin. Here was a man who plucked joy from the mire, made goddesses of peasant girls, and enthroned the honest man. One whose sympathy, with loving arms, embraced all forms of suffering life, who hated slavery of every kind, who was as natural as heaven's blue, with humor kindly as an autumn day, with wit as sharp as Ithuriel's spear, and scorn that blasted like the simoon's breath. A man who loved this world, this life, the things of every day, and placed above all else the thrilling ecstasies of human love.

I read and read again with rapture, tears and smiles, feeling that a great heart was throbbing in the lines.

The religious, the lugubrious, the artificial, the spiritual poets were forgotten or remained only as the fragments, the half remembered horrors of monstrous and distorted dreams.

I had found at last a natural man, one who despised his country's cruel creed, and was brave and sensible enough to say: "All religions are auld wives' fables, but an honest man has nothing to fear, either in this world or the world to come."

One who had the genius to write "Holy Willie's Prayer" — a poem that crucified Calvinism and through its bloodless heart thrust the spear of common sense — a poem that made every orthodox creed the food of scorn — of inextinguishable laughter.

Burns had his faults, his frailties. He was

intensely human. Still, I would rather appear at the "Judgment Seat" drunk, and be able to say that I was the author of "A Man's a Man for A' That," than to be perfectly sober and admit that I had lived and died a Scotch Presbyterian.

And then I read Shakespeare, the plays, the sonnets, the poems — read all. I beheld a new heaven and a new earth; Shakespeare, who knew the brain and heart of man — the hopes and fears, the loves and hatreds, the vices and the virtues of the human race; whose imagination read the tear-blurred records, the blood-stained pages of all the past, and saw falling athwart the outspread scroll the light of hope and love; Shakespeare, who sounded every depth — while on the loftiest peak there fell the shadow of his wings.

I compared the Plays with the "inspired" books — *Romeo and Juliet* with the Song of Solomon, *Lear* with Job, and the Sonnets with the Psalms, and I found that Jehovah did not understand the art of speech. I compared Shakespeare's women — his perfect women — with the women of the Bible. I found that Jehovah was not a sculptor, not a painter — not an artist — that he lacked the power that changes clay to flesh — the art, the plastic touch, that molds the perfect form — the breath that gives it free and joyous life — the genius that creates the faultless.

The sacred books of all the world are worthless dross and common stones compared with Shakespeare's glittering gold and gleaming gems.

I read Voltaire — Voltaire, the greatest man of his century, and who did more for liberty of thought and speech than any other being, human or "divine." Voltaire, who tore the mask from hypocrisy and found behind the painted smile the fangs of hate. Voltaire, who attacked the savagery of the law, the cruel decisions of venal courts, and rescued victims from the wheel and rack. Voltaire, who waged war against the tyranny of thrones, the greed and heartlessness of power. Voltaire, who filled the flesh of priests with the barbed and poisoned arrows of his wit and made the pious jugglers, who cursed him in public, laugh at themselves in private. Voltaire, who sided with the oppressed, rescued the unfortunate, championed the obscure and weak, civilized judges, repealed laws and abolished torture in his native land.

In every direction this tireless man fought the absurd, the miraculous, the supernatural, the idiotic, the unjust. He had no reverence for the ancient. He was not awed by pageantry and pomp, by crowned Crime or mitered Pretence. Beneath the crown he saw the criminal, under the miter, the hypocrite.

To the bar of his conscience, his reason, he summoned the barbarism and the barbarians of his time. He pronounced judgment against them all, and that judgment has been affirmed by the intelligent world. Voltaire lighted a torch and gave to others the sacred flame. The light still shines and will as long as man loves liberty and seeks for truth.

I read Zeno, the man who said, centuries before our Christ was born, that man could not own his fellow-man.

"No matter whether you claim a slave by purchase or capture, the title is bad. They who claim to own their fellow-men, look down into the pit and forget the justice that should rule the world."

I became acquainted with Epicurus, who taught the religion of usefulness, of temperance, of courage and wisdom, and who said: "Why should I fear death? If I am, death is not. If death is, I am not. Why should I fear that which cannot exist when I do?"

I read about Socrates, who when on trial for his life said, among other things, to his judges these wondrous words: "I have not sought during my life to amass wealth and to adorn my body, but I have sought to adorn my soul with the jewels of wisdom, patience, and above all with a love of liberty."

So, I read about Diogenes, the philosopher who hated the superfluous — the enemy of waste and greed, and who one day entered the temple, reverently approached the altar, crushed a louse between the nails of his thumbs, and solemnly said: "The sacrifice of Diogenes to all the gods." This parodied the worship of the world — satirized all creeds, and in one act put the essence of religion.

I compared Zeno, Epicurus and Socrates, three heathen wretches who had never heard of the Old Testament or the Ten Commandments, with Abraham, Isaac and Jacob, three favorites of Jehovah, and I was depraved enough to think that the Pagans were superior to the Patriarchs — and to Jehovah himself.

I do not deny. I do not know — but I do not believe. I believe that the natural is supreme — that from the infinite chain no link can be lost or broken — that there is no supernatural power that can answer prayer — no power that worship can persuade or change — no power that cares for man.

I believe that with infinite arms Nature embraces the all — that there is no interference —

no chance — that behind every event are the necessary and countless causes, and that beyond every event will be and must be the necessary and countless effects.

Man must protect himself. He cannot depend upon the supernatural — upon an imaginary father in the skies. He must protect himself by finding the facts in Nature, by developing his brain, to the end that he may overcome the obstructions and take advantage of the forces of Nature.

Is there a God?

I do not know.

Is man immortal?

I do not know.

One thing I do know, and that is, that neither hope, nor fear, belief, nor denial, can change the fact. It is as it is, and it will be as it must be.

We wait and hope.

ON SUICIDE
— An interview —

QUESTION
Is a suicide necessarily insane?

ANSWER
No. At the same time I believe that a great majority of suicides are insane. There are circumstances under which suicide is natural, sensible and right. When a man is of no use to himself, when he can be of no use to others, when his life is filled with agony, when the future has no promise of relief, then I think he has the right to cast the burden of life away and seek the repose of death.

Is a suicide necessarily a coward?
I cannot conceive of cowardice in connection with suicide. Of nearly all things death is the most feared. And the man who voluntarily enters the realm of death cannot properly be called a coward. Many men who kill themselves forget the duties they owe to others — forget their wives and children. Such men are heartless, wicked, brutal; but they are not cowards.

When is the suicide of the sane justifiable?
To escape death by torture; to avoid being devoured by a cancer; to prevent being a burden on those you love; when you can be of no use to others or to yourself; when life is unbearable; when in all the horizon of the future there is no star of hope.

Do you believe that any suicides have been caused or encouraged by your declaration three years ago that suicide sometimes was justifiable?
Many preachers talk as though I had inaugurated, invented, suicide, as though no one who had not read my ideas on suicide had ever taken his own life. Talk as long as language lasts, you cannot induce a man to kill himself. The man who takes his own life does not go to others to find reasons or excuses.

On the whole is the world made better or worse by suicides?
Better by some and poorer by others.

If suicide is sometimes justifiable, is not killing of born idiots and infants hopelessly handicapped at birth equally so?
There is no relation between the questions — between suicides and killing idiots. Suicide may,

under certain circumstances, be right and killing idiots may be wrong; killing idiots may be right and suicide may be wrong. When we look about us, when we read interviews with preachers about Jonah, we know that all the idiots have not been killed.

SUPERSTITION
— *1887* —

The believers in the supernatural, in a power superior to nature, in God, have what they call "inspired books." These books contain the absolute truth. They must be believed. He who denies them will be punished with eternal pain. These books are not addressed to human reason. They are above reason. They care nothing for what a man calls "facts." Facts that do not agree with these books are mistakes. These books are independent of human experience, of human reason.

Our inspired books constitute what we call the "Bible." The man who reads this inspired book, looking for contradictions, mistakes and interpolations, imperils the salvation of his soul. While he reads he has no right to think, no right to reason. To believe is his only duty.

Millions of men have wasted their lives in the study of this book — in trying to harmonize contradictions and to explain the obscure and seemingly absurd. In doing this they have justified nearly every crime and every cruelty. In its follies they have found the profoundest wisdom. Hundreds of creeds have been constructed from its inspired passages. Probably no two of its readers have agreed as to its meaning. Thousands have studied Hebrew and Greek that they might read the Old and New Testament in the languages in which they were written.

The more they studied, the more they differed.

By the same book they proved that nearly everybody is to be lost, and that all are to be saved; that slavery is a divine institution, and that all men should be free; that polygamy is right, and that no man should have more than one wife; that the powers that be are ordained of God, and that the people have a right to overturn and destroy the powers that be; that all the actions of men were predestined — preordained from eternity, and yet that man is free; that all the heathen will be lost; that all the heathen will be saved; that all men who live according to the light of nature will be damned for their pains; that you must be baptized by sprinkling; that you must he baptized by immersion; that there is no salvation without baptism; that baptism is useless; that you must believe in the Trinity; that it is sufficient to believe in God; that you must believe that a Hebrew peasant was God; that at the same time he was halfman, that he was of the blood of David

through his supposed father Joseph, who was not
his father, and that it is not necessary to believe that
Christ was God; that you must believe that the
Holy Ghost proceeded; that it makes no difference
whether you do or not; that you must keep the
Sabbath holy; that Christ taught nothing of the
kind; that Christ established a church; that he
established no church; that the dead are to he
raised; that there is to be no resurrection; that
Christ is coming again; that he has made his last
visit; that Christ went to hell and preached to the
spirits in prison; that he did nothing of the kind;
that all the Jews are going to perdition; that they are
all going to heaven; that all the miracles described
in the Bible were performed; that some of them
were not, because they are foolish, childish and idiotic; that all the Bible is inspired; that some of the
books are not inspired; that there is to be a general
judgment, when the sheep and goats are to be
divided; that there never will be any general judgment; that the sacramental bread and wine are
changed into the flesh and blood of God and the
Trinity; that they are not changed; that God has no
flesh or blood; that there is a place called "purga-
tory"; that there is no such place; that unbaptized
infants will be lost; that they will be saved; that we

must believe the Apostles' Creed; that the apostles made no creed; that the Holy Ghost was the father of Christ; that Joseph was his father; that the Holy Ghost had the form of a dove; that there is no Holy Ghost; that heretics should be killed; that you must not resist evil; that you should murder unbelievers; that you must love your enemies; that you should take no thought for the morrow, but should be diligent in business; that you should lend to all who ask, and that one who does not provide for his own household is worse than an infidel.

Our God was made by men, sculptured by savages who did the best they could. They made our God somewhat like themselves, and gave to him their passions, their ideas of right and wrong.

As man advanced he slowly changed his God — took a little ferocity from his heart, and put the light of kindness in his eyes. As man progressed he obtained a wider view, extended the intellectual horizon and again he changed his God, making him as nearly perfect as he could, and yet this God was patterned after those who made him. As man became civilized, as he became merciful, he began to love justice, and as his mind expanded his ideal became purer, nobler, and so his God became more merciful, more loving.

As Christians have changed their God, so they have accordingly changed their Bible. The impossible and absurd, the cruel and the infamous, have been mostly thrown aside, and thousands are now engaged in trying to save the inspired word. Of course, the orthodox still cling to every word, and still insist that every line is true. They are literalists. To them the Bible means exactly what it says. They want no explanation. They care nothing for commentators. Contradictions cannot disturb their faith. They deny that any contradictions exist. They loyally stand by the sacred text, and they give it the narrowest possible interpretation. They are like the janitor of an apartment house who refused to rent a flat to a gentleman because he said he had children. "But," said the gentleman, "my children are both married and live in Iowa." "That makes no difference," said the janitor. "I am not allowed to rent a flat to any man who has children."

All the orthodox churches are obstructions on the highway of progress. Every orthodox creed is a chain, a dungeon. Every believer in the "inspired book" is a slave who drives reason from her throne, and in her stead crowns fear.

Reason is the light, the sun of the brain. It is the compass of the mind, the ever-constant Northern

Star, the mountain peak that lifts itself above all clouds.

After all we know but little. In the darkness of life there are a few gleams of light.

Possibly the dropping of a dishcloth prophesies the coming of company, but we have no evidence. Possibly it is dangerous for thirteen to dine together, but we have no evidence. Possibly a maiden's matrimonial chances are determined by the number of seeds in an apple, or by the number of leaves on a flower, but we have no evidence. Possibly certain stones give good luck to the wearer, while the wearing of others brings loss and death. Possibly a glimpse of the new moon over the left shoulder brings misfortune. Possibly there are curative virtues in old bones, in sacred rags and holy hairs, in images and bits of wood, in rusty nails and dried blood, but the trouble is we have no evidence. Possibly comets, eclipses and shooting stars foretell the death of kings, the destruction of nations or the coming of plague. Possibly devils take possession of the bodies and minds of men. Possibly witches, with the Devil's help, control the winds, breed storms on sea and land, fill summer's lap with frosts and snow, and work with charm and spell against the public weal, but of this we have no evidence. It may be that all the miracles described in the Old and New Testament were performed; that the pallid flesh of the dead felt once more the thrill of life; that the corpse arose and felt upon his smiling lips the kiss of wife and child. Possibly water was turned into wine, loaves and fishes increased, and possibly devils were expelled from men and women; possibly fishes were found with money in their mouths; possibly clay and spittle brought back the light to sightless eyes, and possibly words cured disease and made the leper clean, but of this we have no evidence.

A TALE

— 1880 —

There was a Jewish gentleman went into a restaurant to get his dinner, and the devil of temptation whispered in his ear: "Eat some bacon." He knew if there was anything in the universe calculated to excite the wrath of an infinite being, who made every shining star, it was to see a gentleman eating bacon. He knew it, and he knew the infinite being was looking, that he was the eternal eavesdropper of the universe. But his appetite got the better of his conscience, as it often has with us all, and he ate that bacon. He knew it was wrong, and his conscience felt the blood of shame in its cheek. When he went into that restaurant the weather was delightful, the sky was as blue as June, and when he came out the sky was covered with angry clouds, the lightning leaping from one to the other, and the earth shaking beneath the voice of the thunder. He went back into that restaurant with a face as white as milk, and he said to one of the keepers:

"My God, did you ever hear such a fuss about a little piece of bacon?"

FREE SPEECH AND
HONEST TALK

— 1888 —

I am here tonight for the purpose of defending your right to differ with me. I want to convince you that you are under no compulsion to accept my creed; that you are, so far as I am concerned, absolutely free to follow the torch of your reason according to your conscience; and I believe that you are civilized to that degree that you will extend to me the right that you claim for yourselves.

I admit, at the very threshold, that every human being thinks as he must; and the first proposition really is whether man has the right to think. It will bear but little discussion, for the reason that no man can control his thought. If you think you can, what are you going to think tomorrow? What are you going to think next year? If you can absolutely control your thought, can you stop thinking?

The question is, has the will any power over the thought? What is thought? It is the result of nature — of the outer world — first upon the senses — those impressions left upon the brain as pictures of things in the outward world, and these pictures are transformed into, or produce, thought; and as long as the doors of the senses are open, thoughts will be produced. Whoever looks at anything in nature, thinks. Whoever hears any sound — or any symphony — no matter what — thinks. Whoever looks upon the sea, or on a star, or on a flower, or on the face of a fellow-man, thinks, and the result of that look is an absolute necessity. The thought produced will depend upon your brain, upon your experience, upon the history of your life.

One who looks upon the sea, knowing that the one he loved the best had been devoured by its hungry waves, will have certain thoughts; and he who sees it for the first time will have different thoughts. In other words, no two brains are alike; no two lives have been, or are, or ever will be the same. Consequently, nature cannot produce the same effect upon any two brains, or upon any two hearts.

The only reason why we wish to exchange thoughts is that we are different. If we were all the same, we would die dumb. No thought would be expressed after we found that our thoughts were precisely alike. We differ — our thoughts are different. Therefore the commerce that we call conversation.

Each brain is a kind of field where nature sows with careless hands the seeds of thought. Some brains are poor and barren fields, producing weeds and thorns, and some are like the tropic world where grow the palm and pine — children of the sun and soil.

You read Shakespeare. What do you get out of Shakespeare? All that your brain is able to hold. It depends upon your brain. If you are great — if you have been cultivated — if the wings of your imagination have been spread — if you have had great, free, and splendid thoughts — if you have stood upon the edge of things — if you have had the courage to meet all that can come — you get an immensity from Shakespeare. If you have lived nobly — if you have loved with every drop of your blood and every fibre of your being — if you have suffered — if you have enjoyed — then you get an immensity from Shakespeare. But if you have lived a poor, little, mean, wasted, barren, weedy life — you get very little from that immortal man.

So it is from every source in nature — what you get depends upon what you are.

There has always been in men the instinct of self-preservation. There was a time when men believed, and honestly believed, that there was above them a God. Sometimes they believed in many, but it will be sufficient for my illustration to say one. Man believed that there was in the sky above him a God who attended to the affairs of men. He believed that that God, sitting upon his throne, rewarded virtue and punished vice. He believed also that that God held the community responsible for the sins of individuals. He honestly believed it. When the flood came, or when the earthquake devoured, he really believed that some God was filled with anger — with holy indignation — at his children. He believed it, and so he looked about among his neighbors to see who was at fault, and if there was any man who had failed to bring his sacrifice to the altar, had failed to kneel, it may be to the priest, failed to be present in the temple, or had given it as his opinion that the God of that tribe or of that nation was of no use, then, in order to placate the God, they seized the neighbor and sacrificed him on the altar of their ignorance and of their fear.

They believed when the lightning leaped from the cloud and left its blackened mark upon the man, that he had done something — that he had excited the wrath of the gods.

And while man so believed, while he believed

that it was necessary, in order to defend himself to kill his neighbor — he acted simply according to the dictates of his nature.

What I claim is that we have now advanced far enough not only to think, but to know, that the conduct of man has nothing to do with the phenomena of nature. We are now advanced far enough to absolutely know that no man can be bad enough and no nation infamous enough to cause an earthquake. I think we have got to that point that we absolutely know that no man can be wicked enough to entice one of the bolts from heaven — that no man can be cruel enough to cause a drought — and that you could not have infidels enough on the earth to cause another flood. I think we have advanced far enough not only to say that, but to absolutely know it — I mean people who have thought, and in whose minds there is something like reasoning.

We know, if we know anything, that the lightning is just as apt to hit a good man as a bad man. We know it. We know that the earthquake is just as liable to swallow virtue as to swallow vice. And you know just as well as I do that a ship loaded with pirates is just as apt to outride the storm as one crowded with missionaries. You know it.

I am now speaking of the phenomena of nature. I believe, as much as I believe that I live, that the reason a thing is right is because it tends to the happiness of mankind. I believe, as much as I believe that I live, that on the average the good man is not only the happier man, but that no man is happy who is not good. If then we have gotten over that frightful, that awful superstition — we are ready to enjoy hearing the thoughts of each other.

So then, I am simply in favor of intellectual hospitality — that is all. You come to me with a new idea. I invite you into the house. Let us see what you have. Let us talk it over. If I do not like your thought, I will bid it a polite "good day." If I do like it, I will say: "Sit down; stay with me, and become a part of the intellectual wealth of my world." That is all.

And how any human being ever has had the impudence to speak against the right to speak, is beyond the power of my imagination. Here is a man who speaks — who exercises a right that he, by his speech, denies. Can liberty go further than that? Is there any toleration possible beyond the liberty to speak against liberty — the real believer in free speech allowing others to speak against the right to speak? Is there any limitation beyond that?

So, whoever has spoken against the right to speak has admitted that he violated his own doctrine. No man can open his mouth against the freedom of speech without denying every argument he may put forward. Why? He is exercising the right that he denies. How did he get it? Suppose there is one man on an island. You will all admit now that he would have the right to do his own thinking. You will all admit that he has the right to express his thought. Now, will somebody tell me how many men would have to emigrate to that island before the original settler would lose his right to think and his right to express himself?

If there be an infinite Being — and it is a question that I know nothing about — you would he perfectly astonished to know how little I do know on that subject, and yet I know as much as the aggregated world knows, and as little as the smallest insect that ever fanned with happy wings the summer air — if there be such a Being, I have the same right to think that he has simply because it is a necessity of my nature — because I cannot help it. And the Infinite would be just as responsible to the smallest intelligence living in the infinite spaces — he would be just as responsible to that intelligence as that intelligence can be to him, provided that intelligence thinks as a necessity of his nature.

Consequently I simply believe in absolute liberty of mind. And I have no fear about any other world — not the slightest. When I get there, I will give my honest opinion of that country; I will give my honest thought there; and if for that I lose my soul, I will keep at least my self-respect.

ON THE LIFE CYCLE

There is something tenderly appropriate in the serene death of the old. Nothing is more touching than the death of the young, the strong. But when the duties of life have all been nobly done; when the sun touches the horizon; when the purple twilight falls upon the past, the present, and the future; when memory, with dim eyes, can scarcely spell the blurred and faded records of the vanished days — then, surrounded by kindred and by friends, death comes like a strain of music. The day has been long, the road weary, and the traveler gladly stops at the welcome inn.

If we live beyond life's day and reach the dusk, and slowly travel in the shadows of the night, the way seems long, and being weary we ask for rest, and then, as in our youth, we chide the loitering hours. When eyes are dim and memory fails to keep a record of events; when ears are dull and muscles fail to obey the will; when the pulse is low and the tired heart is weak, and the poor brain has hardly power to think, then comes the dream, the hope of rest, the longing for the peace of dreamless sleep.

Quiet, and introspective calm come with the afternoon. Toward evening the mind grows satisfied and still. The flare and flicker of youth are gone, and the soul is like the flame of a lamp where the air is at rest. Age discards the superfluous, the immaterial, the straw and chaff, and hoards the golden grain. The highway is known, and the paths no longer mislead. Clouds are not mistaken for mountains.

The old man has been long at the fair. He is acquainted with the jugglers at the booths. His curiosity has been satisfied. He no longer cares for the exceptional, the monstrous, the marvelous and deformed. He looks through and beyond the gilding, the glitter and gloss, not only of things, but of conduct, of manners, theories, religions and philosophies. He sees clearer. The light no longer shines in his eyes.

Perhaps I have reached the years of discretion. But it may be that discretion is the enemy of happiness. If the buds had discretion there might be no fruit. So it may be that the follies committed in the spring give autumn the harvest.

The falling leaf that tells of autumn's death is, in a subtler sense, a prophecy of spring.

ON LEARNING AND GENIUS

The more a man knows, the more willing he is to learn — the less a man knows, the more positive he is that he knows everything.

The smallest minds mature the earliest. The less there is to a man the quicker he attains his growth. I have known many people who reached their intellectual height while in their mother's arms; I have known people who were exceedingly smart babies to become excessively stupid people. It is with men as with other things. The mullein needs only a year, but the oak a century, and the greatest men are those who have continued to grow as long as they have lived. Small people delight in what they call consistency — that is, it gives them immense pleasure to say that they believe now exactly as they did ten years ago. This simply amounts to a certificate that they have not grown — that they have not developed — and that they know just as little now as they ever did. The highest possible conception of consistency is to be true to the knowledge of today, without the slightest reference to what your opinion was years ago.

There is another view of this subject. Few men have settled opinions before or at thirty. Of course, I do not include persons of genius. At thirty the passions have, as a rule, too much influence; the intellect is not the pilot. At thirty most men have prejudices rather than opinions — that is to say, rather than judgments — and few men have lived to be sixty without materially modifying the opinions they held at thirty.

Talent has the four seasons: spring, that is to say, the sowing of the seeds; summer, growth; autumn, the harvest; winter, intellectual death. But there is now and then a genius who has no winter, and, no matter how many years he may live, on the blossom of his thought no snow falls. Genius has the climate of perpetual growth.

ON LOVE

Love is the only bow on Life's dark cloud. It is the morning and the evening star. It shines upon the babe, and sheds its radiance on the quiet tomb. It is the mother of art, inspirer of poet, patriot and philosopher. It is the air and light of every heart — builder of every home, kindler of every fire on every hearth. It was the first to dream of immortality. It fills the world with melody — for music is the voice of love. Love is the magician, the enchanter, that changes worthless things to Joy, and makes royal kings and queens of common clay. It is the perfume of that wondrous flower, the heart, and without that sacred passion, that divine swoon, we are less than beasts; but with it, earth is heaven, and we are gods.

ON HUMAN HAPPINESS

If upon this earth we ever have a glimpse of heaven, it is when we pass a home in winter, at night, and through the windows, the curtains drawn aside, we see the family about the pleasant hearth; the old lady knitting; the cat playing with the yarn; the children wishing they had as many dolls or dollars or knives or somethings, as there are sparks going out to join the roaring blast; the father reading and smoking, and the clouds rising like incense from the altar of domestic joy. I never passed such a house without feeling that I had received a benediction.

ON SCIENCE AND REASON

To love justice, to long for the right, to love mercy, to pity the suffering, to assist the weak, to forget wrongs and remember benefits — to love the truth, to be sincere, to utter honest words, to love liberty, to wage relentless war against slavery in all its forms, to love wife and child and friend, to make a happy home, to love the beautiful; in art, in nature, to cultivate the mind, to be familiar with the mighty thoughts that genius has expressed, the noble deeds of all the world, to cultivate courage and cheerfulness, to make others happy, to fill life with the splendor of generous acts, the warmth of loving words, to discard error, to destroy prejudice, to receive new truths with gladness, to cultivate hope, to see the calm beyond the storm, the dawn beyond the night, to do the best that can be done and then to be resigned — this is the religion of reason, the creed of science. This satisfies the brain and heart.

ON EVOLUTION

I believe that man came up from the lower animals.
When I first heard of that doctrine I did not like it.
My heart was filled with sympathy for those people
who have nothing to be proud of except ancestors.
I thought, how terrible this will be upon the
nobility of the Old World. Think of their being
forced to trace their ancestry back to the duke
Orang Outang, or to the princess Chimpanzee.
After thinking it all over, I came to the conclusion
that I liked that doctrine.

ON SEPARATION OF CHURCH AND STATE

I have seen a memorial asking that church property be taxed like other property; that no more money should be appropriated from the public treasury for the support of institutions managed by and in the interest of sectarian denominations; for the repeal of all laws compelling the observance of Sunday as a religious day. Such memorials ought to be addressed to the Legislature of all the States. The money of the public should only be used for the benefit of the public. Public money should not be used for what a few gentlemen think is for the benefit of the public. Personally, I think it would be for the benefit of the public to have Infidel or scientific — which is the same thing — lectures delivered in every town, in every State, on every Sunday; but knowing that a great many men disagree with me on this point, I do not claim that such lectures ought to be paid for with public money. The Methodist Church ought not to be sustained by taxation, nor the Catholic, nor any other church. To relieve their property from taxation is to appropriate money, to the extent of that tax, for the support of that church. Whenever a burden is lifted from one piece of property, it is distributed over the rest of the property of the State, and to release one kind of property is to increase the tax on all other kinds.

There was a time when people really supposed that churches were saving souls from the eternal wrath of a God of infinite love. Being engaged in such a philanthropic work, and at that time nobody having the courage to deny it the church being all-powerful — all other property was taxed to support the church; but now the more civilized part of the community, being satisfied that a God of infinite love will not be eternally unjust, feel as though the church should support herself. To exempt the church from taxation is to pay a part of the priest's salary. The Catholic now objects to being taxed to support a school in which his religion is not taught. He is not satisfied with the school that says nothing on the subject of religion. He insists that it is an outrage to tax him to support a school where the teacher simply teaches what he knows. And yet this same Catholic wants his church exempted from taxation, and the tax of an Atheist or of a Jew increased, when he teaches in his untaxed church that the Atheist and Jew will both be eternally damned! Is it possible for impudence to go further?

I insist that no religion should be taught in any school supported by public money; and by religion I mean superstition. Only that should be taught in a school that somebody can learn and that somebody can know. In my judgment, every church should be taxed precisely the same as other property. The church may claim that it is one of the instruments of civilization and therefore should be exempt. If you exempt that which is useful, you exempt every trade and every profession. In my judgment, theaters have done more to civilize mankind than churches; that is to say, theaters have done something to civilize mankind — churches nothing. The effect of all superstition has been to render man barbarous. I do not believe in the civilizing effects of falsehood.

There was a time when ministers were supposed to be in the employ of God, and it was thought that God selected them with great care — that their profession had something sacred about it. These ideas are no longer entertained by sensible people. Ministers should be paid like other professional men, and those who like their preaching should pay for the preach. They should depend, as actors do, upon their popularity, upon the amount of sense, or nonsense, that they have for sale. They should depend upon the market like other people, and if people do not want to hear sermons badly enough to build churches and pay for them, and pay the taxes on them, and hire the preacher, let the money be diverted to some other use. The pulpit should no longer be a pauper. I do not believe in carrying on any business with the contribution box. All the sectarian institutions ought to support themselves. There should be no Methodist or Catholic or Presbyterian hospitals or orphan asylums. All these should be supported by the State. There is no such thing as Catholic charity, or Methodist charity. Charity belongs to humanity, not to any particular form of faith or religion. You will find as many charitable people who never heard of religion, as you can find in any church. The State should provide for those who ought to be provided for. A few Methodists beg of everybody they meet — send women with subscription papers, asking money from all classes of people, and nearly everybody gives something from politeness, or to keep from being annoyed; and when the institution is finished, it is pointed at as the result of Methodism.

Probably a majority of the people in this

country suppose that there was no charity in the world until the Christian religion was founded. Great men have repeated this falsehood, until ignorance and thoughtlessness believe it. There were orphan asylums in China, in India, and in Egypt thousands of years before Christ was born; and there certainly never was a time in the history of the whole world when there was less charity in Europe than during the centuries when the Church of Christ had absolute power. There were hundreds of Mohammedan asylums before Christianity had built ten in the entire world.

All institutions for the care of unfortunate people should be secular — should be supported by the State. The money for the purpose should be raised by taxation, to the end that the burden may be borne by those able to bear it. As it is now, most of the money is paid, not by the rich, but by the generous, and those most able to help their needy fellow citizens are the very ones who do nothing. If the money is raised by taxation, then the burden will fall where it ought to fall, and these institutions will no longer be supported by the generous and emotional, and the rich and stingy will no longer be able to evade the duties of citizenship and humanity.

Now, as to the Sunday laws, we know that they are only spasmodically enforced. Now and then a few people are arrested for selling papers or cigars. Some unfortunate barber is grabbed by a policeman because he has been caught shaving a Christian, Sunday morning. Now and then some poor fellow with a hack, trying to make a dollar or two to feed his horses, or to take care of his wife and children, is arrested as though he were a murderer. But in a few days the public are inconvenienced to that degree that the arrests stop and business goes on in its accustomed channels.

Now and then society becomes so pious, so virtuous, that people are compelled to enter saloons by the back door; others are compelled to drink beer with the front shutters up; but otherwise the stream that goes down the thirsty throats is unbroken. The ministers have done their best to prevent all recreation on the Sabbath. They would like to stop all the boats on the Hudson, and the sea — stop all the excursion trains. They would like to compel every human being that lives in the city of New York to remain within its limits twenty-four hours each Sunday. They hate the parks; they hate music; they hate anything that keeps a man away from church. Most of the churches are empty during the summer, and now most of the ministers leave themselves, and give over the entire city to the Devil and his emissaries. And yet if the ministers had their way, there would be no form of human enjoyment except prayer, signing subscription papers, putting money in contribution boxes, listening to sermons, reading the cheerful histories of the Old Testament, imagining the joys of heaven and the torments of hell. The church is opposed to the theater, is the enemy of the opera, looks upon dancing as a crime, hates billiards, despises cards, opposes roller-skating, and even entertains a certain kind of prejudice against croquet.

ON HIS FRIENDSHIP WITH REVEREND CLARK

— An obituary, 1879 —

Upon the grave of the Reverend Alexander Clark I wish to place one flower. Utterly destitute of cold, dogmatic pride, that often passes for the love of God; without the arrogance of the "elect"; simple, free, and kind — this earnest man made me his friend by being mine. I forgot that he was a Christian, and he seemed to forget that I was not, while each remembered that the other was at least a man.

Frank, candid, and sincere, he practiced what he preached, and looked with the holy eyes of charity upon the failings and mistakes of men. He believed in the power of kindness, and spanned with divine sympathy the hideous gulf that separates the fallen from the pure.

Giving freely to others the rights that he claimed for himself, it never occurred to him that his God hated a brave and honest unbeliever. He remembered that even an Infidel had rights that love respects, that hatred has no saving power, and that in order to be a Christian it is not necessary to become less that a human being. He knew that no one can be maligned into kindness, that epithets cannot convince, that curses are not arguments, and that the finger of scorn never points toward heaven. With the generosity of an honest man, he accorded to all the fullest liberty of thought, knowing, as he did, that in the realm of mind a chain is but a curse.

For this man I felt the greatest possible regard. In spite of the taunts and jeers of his brethren, he publicly proclaimed that he would treat Infidels with fairness and respect; that he would endeavor to convince them by argument and win them with love. He insisted that the God he worshiped loved the well-being even of an Atheist. In this grand position he stood almost alone. Tender, just, and loving where others were harsh, vindictive and cruel, he challenged the admiration of every honest man. A few more such clergymen might drive calumny from the lips of faith and render the pulpit worthy of esteem.

The heartiness and kindness with which this generous man treated me can never be excelled. He admitted that I had not lost, and could not lose, a single right by the expression of my honest thought. Neither did he believe that a servant could win the respect of a generous master by persecuting and maligning those whom the master would willingly forgive.

While this good man was living, his brethren blamed him for having treated me with fairness. But, I trust, now that he has left the shore touched by the mysterious sea that never yet has borne, on any wave, the image of a homeward sail, this crime will be forgiven him by those who still remain to preach the love of God.

His sympathies were not confined within the prison of a creed, but ran out and over the walls like vines, hiding the cruel rocks and rusted bars with leaf and flower. He could not echo with his heart the fiendish sentence of eternal fire. In spite of book and creed, he read "between the lines" the words of tenderness and love, with promises for all the world. Above, beyond, the dogmas of his church — humane even to the verge of heresy — causing some to doubt his love of God because he failed to hate his unbelieving fellow-men, he labored for the welfare of mankind, and to his work gave up his life with all his heart.

ON DISAGREEMENT
— *1880* —

Do not imagine for a moment that I think people who disagree with me are bad people. I admit, and I cheerfully admit, that a very large proportion of mankind, and a very large majority, a vast number are reasonably honest. I believe that most Christians believe what they teach; that most ministers are endeavoring to make this world better. I do not pretend to be better than they are. It is an intellectual question. It is a question, first, of intellectual liberty, and after that, a question to be settled at the bar of human reason. I do not pretend to be better than they are. Probably I am a good deal worse than many of them, but that is not the question. The question is: Bad as I am, have I the right to think? And I think I have for two reasons:

First, I cannot help it. And secondly, I like it.

And let me say here, once for all, that for the man Christ I have infinite respect. Let me say, once for all, that the place where man has died for man is holy ground. And let me say, once for all, that to that great and serene man I gladly pay, I gladly pay, the tribute of my admiration and my tears. He was a reformer in his day. He was an infidel in his time.

AT A CHILD'S GRAVE

— 1882 —

I know how vain it is to gild a grief with words, and yet I wish to take from every grave its fear. Here in this world, where life and death are equal kings, all should be brave enough to meet what all the dead have met. The future has been filled with fear, stained and polluted by the heartless past. From the wondrous tree of life the buds and blossoms fall with ripened fruit, and in the common bed of earth, patriarchs and babes sleep side by side.

Why should we fear that which will come to all that is? We cannot tell, we do not know, which is the greater blessing — life or death. We cannot say that death is not a good. We do not know whether the grave is the end of this life, or the door of another, or whether the night here is not somewhere else a dawn. Neither can we tell which is the more fortunate — the child dying in its mother's arms, before its lips have learned to form a word, or he who journeys all the length of life's uneven road, painfully taking the last slow steps with staff and crutch.

Every cradle asks us "Whence?" and every coffin "Whither?" The poor barbarian, weeping above his dead, can answer these questions just as well as the robed priest of the most authentic creed. The tearful ignorance of the one is as consoling as the learned and unmeaning words of the other. No man, standing where the horizon of a life has touched a grave, has any right to prophesy a future filled with pain and tears.

Maybe death gives all there is of worth to life. If those we press and strain within our arms could never die, perhaps that love would wither from the earth. Maybe this common fate treads out from the paths between our hearts the weeds of selfishness and hate. And I had rather live and love where death is king, than have eternal life where love is not. Another life is nought, unless we know and love again the ones who love us here.

They who stand with breaking hearts around this little grave need have no fear. The larger and the nobler faith in all that is, and is to be, tells us that death, even at its worst, is only perfect rest. We know that through the common wants of life — the needs and duties of each hour — their grief will lessen day by day, until at last this grave will be to them a place of rest and peace — almost of joy. There is for them this consolation: The dead do not suffer. If they live again, their lives will surely be as good as ours. We have no fear. We are all children of the same mother, and the same fate awaits us all. We, too, have our religion, and it is this: Help for the living — Hope for the dead.

HOW TO BE SAVED
— *1880* —

You need not fear the anger of a god that you cannot injure. Rather fear to injure your fellow-men. Do not be afraid of a crime you cannot commit. Rather be afraid of the one that you may commit. The reason that you cannot injure God is that the Infinite is condition-less. You cannot increase or diminish the happiness of any being without changing that being's condition. If God is condition-less, you can neither injure nor benefit him.

They say to me: "What do you propose? You have torn this down, what do you propose to give us in place of it?" I have not torn the good down. I have only endeavored to trample out the ignorant, cruel fires of hell. I do not tear away the passage: "God will be merciful to the merciful." I do not destroy the promise: "If you will forgive others, God will forgive you." I would not for anything blot out the faintest star that shines in the horizon of human despair, nor in the sky of human hope; but I will do what I can to get that infinite shadow out of the heart of man.

"What do you propose in place of this?"

Well, in the first place, I propose good fellow-ship — good friends all around. No matter what we believe, shake hands and let it go. That is your opinion; this is mine: let us be friends. Science makes friends; religion, superstition, makes ene-mies. They say: Belief is important. I say: No, actions are important. Judge by deed, not by creed. Good fellowship — good friends — sincere men and women — mutual forbearance, born of mutual respect.

We have had too many of these solemn people. Whenever I see an exceedingly solemn man, I know he is an exceedingly stupid man. No man of any humor ever founded a religion — never. Humor sees both sides. While reason is the holy light, humor carries the lantern, and the man with a keen sense of humor is preserved from the solemn stu-pidities of superstition. I like a man who has got good feeling for everybody; good fellowship.

I believe in the gospel of cheerfulness, the gospel of Good Nature; the gospel of Good Health. Let us pay some attention to our bodies. Take care of our bodies, and our souls will take care of themselves.

I believe in the gospel of Good Living. You cannot make any god happy by fasting. Let us have good food, and let us have it well cooked — and it is a thousand times better to know how to cook than it is to understand any theology in the world.

I believe in the gospel of good clothes; I believe in the gospel of good houses; in the gospel of water and soap. I believe in the gospel of intelligence; in the gospel of education. The schoolhouse is my cathedral. The universe is my Bible. I believe in that gospel of Justice, that we must reap what we sow.

I do not believe in forgiveness as it is preached by the church. We do not need the forgiveness of God, but of each other and of ourselves. If I rob Mr. Smith and God forgives me, how does that help Smith? If I, by slander, cover some poor girl with the leprosy of some imputed crime, and she withers away like a blighted flower and afterward I get the forgiveness of God, how does that help her? If there is another world, we have got to settle with the people we have wronged in this. No bankrupt court there. Every cent must be paid.

For every crime you commit you must answer to yourself and to the one you injure. And if you have ever clothed another with woe, as with a garment of pain, you will never be quite as happy as though you had not done that thing. No forgiveness by the gods. Eternal, inexorable, everlasting justice, so far as Nature is concerned. You must reap the result of your acts. Even when forgiven by the one you have injured, it is not as though the injury had not been done. That is what I believe in. And if it goes hard with me, I will stand it, and I will cling to my logic, and I will bear it like a man.

I believe in the gospel of Intelligence. That is the only lever capable of raising mankind. Intelligence must be the savior of this world. Humanity is the grand religion, and no God can put a man in hell in another world, who has made a little heaven in this. God cannot make a man miserable if that man has made somebody else happy. God cannot hate anybody who is capable of loving anybody. Humanity — that word embraces all there is.

As long as we love we will hope to live, and when the one dies that we love we will say: "Oh, that we could meet again," and whether we do or not it will not be the work of theology. It will be a fact in nature. I would not for my life destroy one star of human hope, but I want it so that when a poor woman rocks the cradle and sings a lullaby to the dimpled darling, she will not be compelled to believe that ninety-nine chances in a hundred she is raising kindling wood for hell.

One world at a time is my doctrine. It is said in this Testament, "Sufficient unto the day is the evil thereof"; and I say: Sufficient unto each world is the evil thereof.

And suppose after all that death does end all. Next to eternal joy, next to being forever with those we love and those who have loved us, next to that, is to be wrapped in the dreamless drapery of eternal peace. Next to eternal life is eternal sleep. Upon the shadowy shore of death the sea of trouble casts no wave. Eyes that have been curtained by the everlasting dark, will never know again the burning touch of tears. Lips touched by eternal silence will never speak again the broken words of grief. Hearts of dust do not break. The dead do not weep. Within the tomb no veiled and weeping sorrow sits, and in the rayless gloom is crouched no shuddering fear.

I had rather think of those I have loved, and lost, as having returned to earth, as having become a part of the elemental wealth of the world — I would rather think of them as unconscious dust, I would rather dream of them as gurgling in the streams, floating in the clouds, bursting in the foam of light upon the shores of worlds, I would rather think of them as the lost visions of a forgotten night, than to have even the faintest fear that their naked souls have been clutched by an orthodox god. I will leave my dead where nature leaves them. Whatever flower of hope springs up in my heart I will cherish, I will give it breath of sighs and rain of tears. But I cannot believe that there is any being in this universe who has created a human soul for eternal pain. I would rather that every god would destroy himself; I would rather that we all should go to eternal chaos, to black and starless night, than that just one soul should suffer eternal agony.

I have made up my mind that if there is a God, he will be merciful to the merciful.

Upon that rock I stand.

That he will not torture the forgiving.

Upon that rock I stand.

That every man should be true to himself, and that there is no world, no star, in which honesty is a crime.

Upon that rock I stand.

The honest man, the good woman, the happy child, have nothing to fear, either in this world or the world to come.

Upon that rock I stand.

A FABLE

— *1878* —

A devout clergyman sought every opportunity to impress upon the mind of his son the fact that God takes care of all his creatures.

Happening, one day, to see a crane wading in quest of food, the good man pointed out to his son the perfect adaptation of the crane to get his living in that manner. "See," said he, "how his legs are formed for wading! What a long slender bill he has! Observe how nicely he folds his feet when putting them in or drawing them out of the water! He does not cause the slightest ripple. He is thus enabled to approach the fish without giving them any notice of his arrival."

"My son," said he, "it is impossible to look at that bird without recognizing the design, as well as the goodness of God, in thus providing the means of subsistence."

"Yes," replied the boy. "I think I see the goodness of God, at least so far as the crane is concerned. But after all, father, don't you think the arrangement a little tough on the fish?"

ACKNOWLEDGMENTS

Thanks to Chip Fleischer and Kristin Sperber at Steerforth Press, and to Roger E. Greeley, Melanie Jackson, and Vanessa Weeks Page.

All love and gratitude to Julieta Stack Page.

Credits

Creed: From a recording of Ingersoll's voice made by Thomas Edison in 1882. It can be heard at www.secularhumanism.org/ingersoll/creed.ram.

Centennial Oration: An address delivered in Peoria, Illinois, on July 4, 1876. Reprinted from volume nine of the Dresden Edition.

God in the Constitution: Originally published in *The Arena*, Boston, Massachusetts, 1890. Reprinted in volume eleven of the Dresden Edition.

A Christmas Sermon: Originally published in the *New York Evening Telegram*, December 19, 1891. Reprinted in volume seven of the Dresden Edition.

The Liberty of Man, Woman and Child: A lecture first delivered in 1877. Reprinted from volume one of the Dresden Edition.

On Freethought: Adapted from "Has Freethought a Constructive Side?" originally published in *The Truth Seeker* in 1890; reprinted in volume eleven of the Dresden Edition.

Thomas Paine: Written in 1870, it was originally published in *The Gods and Other Lectures* (Peoria, Ill.: C. P. Farrell, 1878). reprinted in volume one of the Dresden Edition.

On Lent: Adapted from an interview entitled "Beaconsfield, Lent and Revivals" published in the *Brooklyn Eagle*, April 24, 1881. Reprinted in volume eight of the Dresden Edition.

On Republicanism: Reprinted from an "Address to the Business Men of New York," delivered in 1880 and originally printed in the *New York Tribune*. Reprinted from *The Complete Lectures of Col. R. G. Ingersoll*.

Abraham Lincoln: An excerpt from "The Liberty of Man, Woman and Child," a lecture first delivered in 1877. Reprinted from volume one of the Dresden Edition.

Why I Am an Agnostic: A lecture first delivered in 1896. Reprinted from volume four of the Dresden Edition.

Suicide and Sanity: From an 1897 interview published in the *New York Press*. Reprinted from volume seven of the Dresden Edition.

Superstition: A lecture delivered in 1898. Reprinted from volume four of the Dresden Edition.

A Tale: Adapted from "What Must We Do to Be Saved?" a lecture delivered in 1880. Reprinted from volume one of the Dresden Edition.

Free Speech and Honest Talk: Adapted from "The Limits of Toleration," a lecture delivered at the Metropolitan Opera House in New York, May 8, 1888. Reprinted from volume seven of the Dresden Edition.

On the Life Cycle and On Learning and Genius: Adapted from "Fragments of Ingersoll," collected by Eva A. Ingersoll and Susan Farrell and printed in volume twelve of the Dresden Edition.

On Love: Adapted from "Orthodoxy," a lecture delivered in 1884. Reprinted from volume two of the Dresden Edition.

ACKNOWLEDGMENTS

On Human Happiness: Adapted from "The Liberty of Man, Woman and Child," a lecture first delivered in 1877. Reprinted from volume one of the Dresden Edition.

On Science and Reason: Adapted from "The Foundations of Faith," a lecture delivered in 1895. Reprinted from volume four of the Dresden Edition.

On Evolution: Adapted from "The Liberty of Man, Woman and Child," a lecture first delivered in 1877. Reprinted from volume one of the Dresden Edition.

On Separation of Church and State: Adapted from "Some Live Topics," an interview originally published in *The Truth Seeker* on September 5, 1885. Reprinted from volume eight of the Dresden Edition.

On His Friendship with Reverend Clark: Adapted from "A Tribute to Reverend Alexander Clark," an address delivered on July 13, 1879. Reprinted from volume twelve of the Dresden Edition.

On Disagreement: Adapted from "What Must We Do to Be Saved?" a lecture delivered in 1880. Reprinted from volume one of the Dresden Edition.

At a Child's Grave: Delivered at the funeral of Harry Miller, January 8, 1882, in Washington, D.C. Reprinted from volume twelve of the Dresden Edition.

How to Be Saved: Adapted from "What Must We Do to Be Saved?" a lecture delivered in 1880. Reprinted from volume one of the Dresden Edition.

A Fable: Adapted from "The Gods," originally published in *The Gods and Other Lectures* (Peoria, Ill: C. P. Farrell, 1878). Reprinted from volume one of the Dresden Edition.

BIBLIOGRAPHY

Greeley, Roger, editor. *Ingersoll: Immortal Infidel.* Buffalo, N.Y. : Prometheus Books, 1977.

Ingersoll, Robert G. *The Complete Lectures of Col. R. G. Ingersoll.* Chicago, Ill.: Regan Publishing, 1926.

————. *The Works of Robert G. Ingersoll,* Dresden edition. 12 volumes. New York: C. P. Farrell, 1900.

Jacoby, Susan. *Freethinkers: A History of American Secularism.* New York: Metropolitan Books, 2004.

Larson, Orvin Prentiss. *American Infidel: Robert G. Ingersoll.* New York: Citadel Press, 1962.